CONDITIONING FOR BASKETBALL

A GUIDE FOR COACHES AND ATHLETES

- **Step-by-step instructions on how to develop fitness for basketball.**

The University of
South Carolina's

Bill Foster

LEISURE PRESS

A publication of Leisure Press.
P.O. Box 3, West Point, N.Y. 10996
Copyright © 1983 by Leisure Press
All rights reserved. Printed in the U.S.A.

ISBN: 0-918438-79-9
Library of Congress Number: 81-82403

Front cover photo: David Madison
Text action photos: Bill Cain
Text instructional photos: Bill Cain, David Goldner, Janeart Inc., and
    Tim Kearin.

Color photos by Manuel Gaetan, Bill Cain, USC Information Services, and
    the South Carolina Department of Parks, Recreation and Tourism.

CONTENTS

Assistant Coach

Ray Jones (LaSalle '69). A native of Clifton, N.J., he received the Bachelor of Arts degree in Political Science from LaSalle and also earned the Master of Arts in Physical Education from the University of Houston. He coached at Jacksonville, Houston, Cincinnati, Duke and Furman Universities before joining the South Carolina staff in March 1980.

Trainer

Jim Price is athletic trainer for Gamecock basketball as well as for the spring sports teams. A native of Texas, Price joined the South Carolina staff in 1959 and the basketball team's Far East tour will be his third experience with international competition. Price served as trainer for the United States team in the 1967 Pan American games and was the American trainer in an International AAU basketball tournament in Italy in 1971.

7

Most successful athletes are successful because they make a sincere commitment to personal excellence and then work hard enough to achieve their goals.

1
BE PREPARED

"Conditioning and fundamentals go hand in hand."
John Wooden
Former Coach, UCLA
Six-time NCAA Champions

W hat does it take to be a winner? Some coaches and athletes might answer this question by responding that in order to be a winner a player has to possess unique physical (genetic) characteristics, such as being very tall or extremely quick. Others feel that the key to being a winner is the ability to learn as much as you can about each aspect of the game.

In fact the answer lies somewhere between the two extremes (genetic versus technical). Not everyone can be 7′2″ or the quickest 6′1″ guard in the world. On the other hand, all of the technical knowledge in the world relating to how to play basketball is virtually useless if the player is either unwilling or incapable of applying that knowledge where it counts—**ON THE COURT**.

The impetus behind most successful athletes is twofold. **First**, the individual must make a personal commitment to excellence in his chosen endeavor. This involves identifying what it takes to be a winner in his sport and focusing his mental and physical energies towards accomplishing each of the various steps. Mentally, the athlete must be alert at all times. He must concentrate on developing "winning habits". There is no substitute for hustle, aggressive play, and concentrating wholly on the job to be done. Physically, the athlete should always be in the best possible shape. Not only does this require that he develop his muscles and stamina to high levels but also that he be well rested and adhere to sound nutritional principles.

Be Prepared

The **second** step is hard work. Once a commitment is made, it takes hard work to ensure that the athlete's goals are achieved. Achieving those goals must be the first priority. For most individuals, this requires many long hours and a considerable expenditure of both time and energy. While an average athlete is often willing to just "get by", the winning athlete will accept nothing less than his very best effort. When he steps on the court, he has literally and figuratively "paid the price of success". More simply stated, he is **prepared to be a winner**.

Toward that end, I have 23 "axioms of success" which over the years I have always attempted to encourage my players to be aware of and ascribe to:

1. Good things come to him who waiteth, if he worketh like heck while he waiteth.
2. At birth we inherit a half million—not dollars, but hours; it's how *you* invest it that counts.
3. The player makes the team . . . the team makes the player.
4. Take what you have and make it better.
5. Defense . . . no glory, just wins.
6. Nothing worth doing is easy; but nothing worth doing is impossible if you develop a winning, hard-working attitude.
7. Defense is a condition of the mind; an attitude of mental toughness combined with aggressiveness and a willingness to work hard.
8. The winner is always part of the answer. The loser is always part of the problem.
9. Plan your work; work your plan.
10. Proper habits provide the opportunity for greatness.
11. A winner makes commitments . . . a loser makes promises.
12. The winner always has a program. The loser always has an excuse.
13. The scoreboard is more important than the scorebook.
14. No one ever drowned in sweat.
15. Take nothing for granted—don't assume.
16. There is no detail too small.
17. It's amazing how much can be accomplished if no one cares who gets the credit.
18. The only place where success comes before work is in the dictionary.
19. No one knows what he can do till he tries.
20. Don't ever think that you're so good that you can get by with less than your best. No one ever was, or ever will be that good.
21. Work well begun is half done.
22. The road to success is no thruway.
23. The winner says "it may be difficult, but it's possible." The loser says, "it may be possible, but it's too difficult."

So BE READY! Commit yourself to excellence and work hard to achieve your goals. Be prepared to be a winner.
IT'S UP TO YOU . . . . .

2
CONDITIONING:
THE WINNING EDGE

Without exception, a more physically fit athlete is a better athlete. While most coaches and athletes believe it, too few take the time and energy to implement this fundamental concept into their overall efforts to become a champion. These people feel that basketball is such a vigorous sport that merely playing the game will get them into top condition. Such individuals claim that they don't have enough time . . . enough sufficient equipment . . . in comparison to other things which need to be done, conditioning isn't that important enough . . . etc. What these individuals fail to understand is that regardless of the sport, a higher level of physical fitness will benefit **any athlete**. The list of benefits is almost endless—a stronger athlete will be able to run faster, jump higher, throw more forcefully, be less susceptible to injury, be more able to sustain his level of performance for a longer period of time, etc.

It is hardly surprising (for example) that some coaches are very "uncomfortable" with the thought of having their players lift weights. Incorrectly, they believe that lifting weights will make their athletes muscle-bound, negatively effect their shooting skills, and generally waste their time. Since most basketball coaches have had **little** or **no** experience with lifting weights (either as a coach or during their days as an athlete), they conclude that strength training is neither necessary or worthwhile. Nothing could be further from the truth. A higher level of muscular fitness will have a positive effect on almost every skill it takes to be a successful basketball player (shooting, rebounding, passing, etc.). Athletes who don't lift weights who are considered highly skilled in their particular sport are not successful because they didn't lift weights but **in spite of it**.

A high level of fitness will pay results where they count—*on the basketball court*.

The main point that this book will hopefully make to the reader is that: **Conditioning can make a difference**. How often is a close game decided on a single rebound or loose ball? Late in a game in an intensely contested matchup, more often than not the more physically fit athlete will be able to jump higher, hold onto the ball more forcefully, have the stamina to go after an errant pass, exert the necessary second effort, etc. Perhaps even more importantly, how many athletes have been forced to miss one or more games because of an injury—an injury which might have been avoided had the individual been more physically fit?

While not every young man has the genetic potential to be a Julius Irving, a Mike Gminski, a Gene Banks, or a Larry Bird, every athlete owes it to himself and to his team to develop his physical abilities to their maximum potential. An integral aspect of the developmental process must be a personal commitment to a sound conditioning program. A high level of fitness will pay results where they count—**on the basketball court**.

I strongly advise any athlete interested in developing to his fullest physical potential to focus his efforts on engaging in a properly conducted conditioning program. Not only will it enable him to be a better athlete, it will provide him with "**the winning edge**" to success.

3
HOW TO ORGANIZE YOUR CONDITIONING PROGRAM

Many techniques and methods exist for developing fitness, some more effective than others. The best approach is for every coach and athlete to commit themselves to a conditioning program which is based upon sound, scientifically-proven principles. While differences will sometimes exist between the specific steps taken to implement these principles because of situational differences between schools and colleges, the need to adhere to proper training principles remains constant. Strict adherence to proper training principles and guidelines is a far more critical factor in obtaining maximum improvement than the tools used to develop the various components of fitness. Certainly, no one could deny that some tools are more effective in helping an athlete become physically fit than others. The point to remember, however, is that the lack of any particular piece of equipment is **not** a valid excuse for ignoring any aspect of fitness. Every coach and athlete should analyze their specific situation and, depending upon what tools are available to them, should identify a conditioning program which is appropriate for their situation and which will work for them. What I have done in this book is to present what I believe is the most efficient and effective way of training.

PHYSICAL FITNESS FOR BASKETBALL

For a basketball player, physical fitness can be defined as:

"... The capacity to play basketball at a reasonably intense level for an extended period of time."

This definition implies that for a basketball player being physically fit involves more than either the capacity to carry out normal, every-day physically non-demanding tasks or the capability of playing basketball at a vigorous level of intensity for only a brief period of time. Basketball is a physically

15

demanding game which requires a relatively high level of fitness for the **entire** game for WINNING basketball.

THE COMPONENTS OF PHYSICAL FITNESS

There are five components basic to physical fitness:

• **Cardiovascular Fitness** is that aspect of fitness which enables an individual to engage in strenuous activity for extended periods of time. Dependent upon the combined efficiency of the heart, circulatory vessels, and lungs, cardiovascular fitness is an integral factor in an athlete's performance in sports which involves the use of much of the body's large musculature (e.g. basketball, soccer, and football). The reason for this is that sports in which the large muscles of the body are extensively utilized require that the heart, lungs, and circulatory vessels operate at greater than usual levels of efficiency. When an athlete's circulatory and respiratory systems fail to meet the cardiovascular demands of the sport, performance suffers. Many coaches and athletes refer to cardiovascular fitness as either "stamina" or "wind."

• **Muscular Endurance*** is that aspect of muscular fitness which enables an athlete to engage in localized muscle group activities (e.g. shooting a basketball) for an extended period of time with relative, comparable effectiveness.

• **Muscular Strength** is the maximum amount of force that can be exerted by a muscle or muscle group and is related to the nature of the resistance—that is, whether it is movable (dynamic or isotonic) or fixed (isometric). Two prime examples of basketball skills involving "dynamic muscular strength" are vertical jumping and pulling the ball away from an opponent who is holding it.

• **Flexibility** is the functional capacity of a joint to move through a normal range of motion. It is specific to given joints and is dependent primarily on the musculature surrounding a joint. Figures 3-1 and 3-2 illustrate the "normal" range of motion for the majority of the joints in the body. Both common sense and recent research lend credence to the importance of flexibility

---

*Some exercise physiologists group both muscular endurance and muscular strength into a single component of fitness which they refer to as "muscular fitness." These individuals define muscular fitness as that quality of fitness which enables an individual to engage in activities requiring greater-than-normal levels of muscular development. These individuals claim that muscular development is inclusive in that it encompasses both of the two basic applications of muscular work—endurance and force. Other individuals argue that although the ability to persist in a localized muscle group activity (endurance) and the ability to exert force (strength) are interrelated, the two factors are separate, distinct qualities of fitness.

to basketball players particularly in the reduction of the possibility of injuries. A dramatic illustration of the importance of flexibility in basketball is provided by the photo below.

● **Body Composition** is an indicator of the amount of fat stored in the body. It is an important quality of fitness for the athlete because there is considerable evidence that excess fat stored in the body limits an athlete's performance. Normal values of fat as a percentage of total body weight vary between men and women. The **upper** limit of "normal" for men is 18% and for women 28%. There are no established minimal levels for body fat. If an athlete receives adequate nutrition, it is not possible to be **too** lean. Different sports require varying proportions of body fat for maximum performance. A minimum amount of body fat (10% or less) is desirable for basketball. In almost every sport (with the possible exception of distance swimming), excessive body fat greatly hinders performance.

A high level of flexibility will reduce an athlete's chances of being injured.

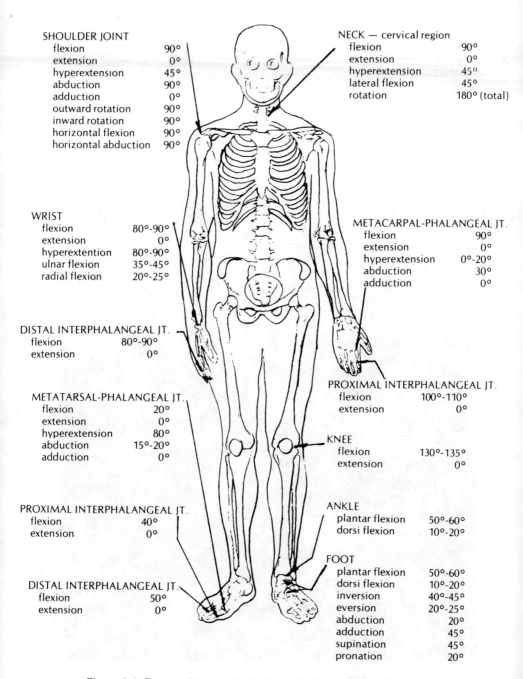

SHOULDER JOINT
flexion	90°
extension	0°
hyperextension	45°
abduction	90°
adduction	0°
outward rotation	90°
inward rotation	90°
horizontal flexion	90°
horizontal abduction	90°

NECK — cervical region
flexion	90°
extension	0°
hyperextension	45°
lateral flexion	45°
rotation	180° (total)

WRIST
flexion	80°-90°
extension	0°
hyperextention	80°-90°
ulnar flexion	35°-45°
radial flexion	20°-25°

METACARPAL-PHALANGEAL JT.
flexion	90°
extension	0°
hyperextension	0°-20°
abduction	30°
adduction	0°

DISTAL INTERPHALANGEAL JT.
flexion	80°-90°
extension	0°

METATARSAL-PHALANGEAL JT.
flexion	20°
extension	0°
hyperextension	80°
abduction	15°-20°
adduction	0°

PROXIMAL INTERPHALANGEAL JT.
flexion	100°-110°
extension	0°

KNEE
flexion	130°-135°
extension	0°

PROXIMAL INTERPHALANGEAL JT.
flexion	40°
extension	0°

ANKLE
plantar flexion	50°-60°
dorsi flexion	10°-20°

DISTAL INTERPHALANGEAL JT.
flexion	50°
extension	0°

FOOT
plantar flexion	50°-60°
dorsi flexion	10°-20°
inversion	40°-45°
eversion	20°-25°
abduction	20°
adduction	45°
supination	45°
pronation	20°

Figure 3-1. Range of motion for fundamental movements: anterior view.

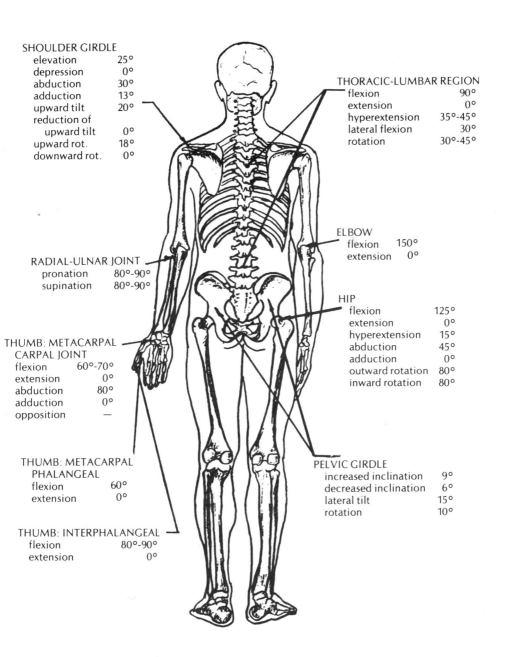

SHOULDER GIRDLE
elevation	25°
depression	0°
abduction	30°
adduction	13°
upward tilt	20°
reduction of	
upward tilt	0°
upward rot.	18°
downward rot.	0°

THORACIC-LUMBAR REGION
flexion	90°
extension	0°
hyperextension	35°-45°
lateral flexion	30°
rotation	30°-45°

ELBOW
flexion	150°
extension	0°

RADIAL-ULNAR JOINT
pronation	80°-90°
supination	80°-90°

HIP
flexion	125°
extension	0°
hyperextension	15°
abduction	45°
adduction	0°
outward rotation	80°
inward rotation	80°

THUMB: METACARPAL CARPAL JOINT
flexion	60°-70°
extension	0°
abduction	80°
adduction	0°
opposition	—

THUMB: METACARPAL PHALANGEAL
flexion	60°
extension	0°

PELVIC GIRDLE
increased inclination	9°
decreased inclination	6°
lateral tilt	15°
rotation	10°

THUMB: INTERPHALANGEAL
flexion	80°-90°
extension	0°

Figure 3-2. Range of motion for fundamental movements: posterior view.

EVALUATING PHYSICAL FITNESS

Generally speaking, an athlete can evaluate his existing overall level of fitness by determining his fitness level on each of the basic aspects of fitness: cardiovascular fitness, endurance, strength, flexibility, and body composition. Each component of physical fitness can be tested by means of simple non-laboratory measures.

The most practical non-laboratory tests of **cardiovascular fitness** are Kenneth H. Cooper's (**Aerobics, The New Aerobics**) twelve-minute field test and modifications of what is known as a step test. In Cooper's 12 minute test, the athlete runs as far as he can in 12 minutes. In approximately 1/4-mile yardage increments, ranging from 1-3/4 miles for excellent to less than 1 mile for very poor, individuals are ranked as having an excellent, good, average, poor, or very poor level of cardiovascular fitness.

In the step test, the individual alternately steps up and down at a specific cadence on a bench (or similar device) which can range in height from 12" to 20". The stepping goes on for a specific period of time and then the post-stepping heart rate is determined to estimate the athlete's adaptation to the demands placed on his cardiovascular system. For the most widely used step test (Harvard), the following scoring formula has been developed:

$$\text{Physical Efficiency Index} = \frac{\text{Duration of exercise in seconds} \times 100}{5.5 \text{X pulse count take 1 to 1-1/2 minutes after the stepping has finished}}$$

The following norms are usually arbitrarily used for evaluation:

Below 50 .... Poor
50-80 .... Average
Above 80 .... Good

Regardless of what step test is used or what normative system of evaluation is employed, all testing conditions should be standardized (time, bench height, cadence, length of the test, etc.). Pulse count is taken by placing the fingers either on the radial pulse (wrist) or on the carotid pulse (slight pressure to the left or right of the Adam's apple).

Muscular endurance is measured by the individual working against a resistance representing less than his level of maximal strength. Isotonic (moving as opposed to static or isometric) endurance is usually tested by using the person's own body weight as the resistance. The most commonly employed endurance tests are pull-ups, chin-ups, sit-ups, and dips. Table 3-1 lists an arbitrary performance rating for these items.

	Pull-ups	Chin-ups	Sit-ups	Dips (1 minute)
Excellent	12+	14+	68+	25+
Good	9-11	10-13	52-67	18-24
Average	6-8	6-9	36-51	9-17
Poor	3-5	3-5	29-35	4-8
Very Poor	0-2	0-2	0-28	0-3

Table 3-1. Normative scale for selective muscular endurance items. (Note: all scores are for men only; physical fitness testing "experts" have so **underestimated** the physical capabilities of athletically inclined women that the existing norms for women are apparently highly inaccurate)

You can take your pulse count by placing your fingers either on your wrist (the radial pulse) or on the side—right or left—of your Adam's apple (the carotid pulse).

In theory, vertical jumping the first time in a game is primarily a function of strength; repeated vertical jumping involves muscular endurance. In reality, it is highly difficult, if not impossible, to identify which factor is more important —strength or endurance. *Both* are critical to the successful basketball player.

Isotonic (moving) strength is tested by determining how much resistance (weight) a given muscle group can move through the full range of joint motion. Numerous mechanical and operational differences between the various types of weight training equipment (Nautilus, Universal, and free weight) make it completely **impossible** to compare strength measurements between the different types of equipment even though the same muscle group may be involved. Given the anatomical and neurological differences between individuals, a listing of the numerous norms for the various muscle groups would be relatively useless. One example of such an artibrary norm is that an individual should be able to standing (military) press a weight equal to at least his own body weight in order to be considered to have above-average strength in the deltoids and triceps.

Isometric strength is measured by quantifying the amount of force an individual can exert against a fixed object. A dynamotor is usually used for this purpose. Since basketball is an action-packed sport involving dynamic movements, a coach would have no practical use for a measurement of an athlete's isometric strength level.

Flexibility is specific to a particular joint. As such, there is no single test which provides information about the flexibility of all the major joints of the body. An athlete may be flexible in one area of the body and relatively inflexible in another. The flexibility requirements for effective performance in an activity vary not only from sport to sport but also from individual to individual. An example of a commonly used flexibility test is the trunk flexion test. Normally scored in inches (plus below the line, minus above the line), the average for college-age men is +1" (+4" for women).

There are no practical, relatively accurate non-laboratory methods of measuring **body composition**. Two tests which will provide an athlete with an estimation of body fat are the "pinch test" and the overweight index (OWI). The "pinch test" involves pinching the skin at selected areas of the body. Since body fat tends to be deposited in certain areas of the body (as opposed to being evenly distributed), the "pinch test" gives a rough indication of the amount of fat collected in a given area. To administer the "pinch test", the individual pinches his skin using his thumb and index finger. If the amount of skin between his fingers is greater than 1", then the individual has an **excessive** amount of fat deposited in that area. One-half to one inch is considered to be too much but **moderate**; while less than a 1/2" pinch of fat is judged to be an **acceptable** amount of fat. The five areas of the body which are usually measured are the triceps, the abdominal area surrounding the "belly-button", the lateral abdominal area (trunk), the inside of the upper thigh area, and the area at the bottom of the pectoralis (chest) muscles. In recent years, a relatively inexpensive ($9.95 approximately) set of plastic skin calipers have been marketed which can measure skin folds much more accurately than the "pinch test."

For the coach who is looking for a formula which will provide him with an indication of whether or not his ball players are "over fat", the overweight index is recommended. The formula for the OWI is:

OWI = 100 × bodyweight (kilograms) ÷ height (centimeters) − 100

An OWI score in excess of 110 represents an extremely high (and counterproductive) level of body fat.

A coach can use skin calipers (more accurate) or the pinch test (less accurate) to determine how much fat has been accumulated in certain areas of his athlete's body.

PLANNING A CONDITIONING PROGRAM

The development of an effective conditioning program requires that a coach answer three basic questions about his athletes: What is their existing level of fitness?; What level of fitness do I want them to achieve?; and How can my team most effectively attain its fitness goals? Honest, accurate responses to these questions will enable your team to undertake a more productive conditioning program.

Specific suggestions for developing a program for each of the components of fitness are presented in Chapters 4-7. Particular attention should be paid, not only to the programs listed for each component, but also to the scientific principles (specific to each component) which must be followed if maximum improvement is to occur. One final consideration of great importance in planning a conditioning program is that each coach should establish his priorities as to what areas of improvement his team needs and what aspects he wishes to emphasize. He should then plan accordingly, given the amount of practice time available, non-practice time available, etc.

THE TWO MOST IMPORTANT GUIDELINES
FOR DEVELOPING FITNESS

In order for a coach or athlete to get the **most** out of his conditioning efforts, he must strictly adhere to two basic principles: demand and specificity.

Demand expresses the principle that in order for substantial improvement to occur in a system of the body or in a quality of physical fitness, the system must be stressed beyond its normal limits. If a demand is not placed on a system, no improvement will occur in that system. For example, a basketball player who can curl 80 lbs. will not improve the strength of his biceps muscles by curling 50 lbs. By the same token, a five minute miler will not break the five-minute barrier by practicing six-minute miles. Physiological responses occur within the body because of a particular need for that response. If an athlete wants the stamina to go "full speed" during a basketball game for 40 minutes, he will not fully develop that capability by only playing in 2 minute increments.

Specificity expresses the principle that "you get what you work for." For the athlete who wishes to improve a specific skill or capability (e.g. vertical jump), the best method is to practice that activity. In other words, nothing replaces the activity itself for the athlete who wishes to improve his ability to perform the activity. This is not to insinuate, however, that no benefit can be derived from non-specific acts of personal conditioning. In the instance of vertical jumping, we advise our athletes to (1) develop the muscles involved in jumping and (2) practice jumping.

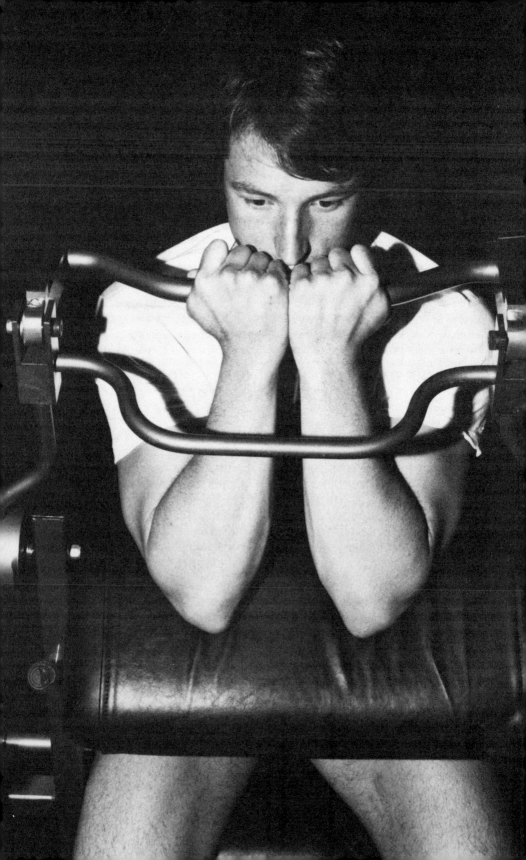

4
STRENGTH TRAINING: FUNDAMENTALS AND TECHNIQUES*

The most integral requirement for developing muscular fitness in the most effective and efficient manner possible is to learn and adhere to the basic skills and guidelines attendant to a properly conducted strength training program. Strict adherence to specific fundamental precepts will enable athletes to accomplish two goals: (1) maximize their gains in muscular fitness and (2) train in as safe a manner as is possible.

MUSCLE SIZE AND STRENGTH

When a demand is placed on a muscle, the muscle responds to the resultant stress by growing in size. This increase in size is also referred to as "hypertrophying." This growth is the result of an increase in the size (**not the number**) of the individual fibers and the tissue (fascia) which surrounds the fibers. The strength of a muscle is roughly proportional to its cross-sectional area. All other factors being equal, the larger a muscle, the stronger a muscle.

WARM-UP

Although contradictory information exists regarding the possible benefits of a warming- or limbering-up before training with weights, common sense strongly suggests that some effort should be devoted to a warm-up period if for no other than safety reasons. Since warming-up produces an increase in the internal temperature of the body, which in turn affects the elasticity and extensibility of the involved muscle tissue, the athlete who "warms-up" before engaging in rigorous activity is generally believed to be less prone to muscle pulls, tears, etc. The length of the warm-up period and the activities

---

*Much of the information which appears in this chapter is based on material found in *Conditioning for a Purpose: The West Point Way* (Dr. James A. Peterson, editor) 2nd edition, 1982. Used by permission of the publisher, Leisure Press, West Point, New York 10996.

to be followed depend on the individual. For most athletes, five to ten minutes of libering-up should suffice. Suggested warm-up activities include: jumping-jacks, running-in-place, and lifting **light** weights through the ranges of motion specific to the exercises in the weight training program.

PROPER LIFTING TECHNIQUES

A complete mastery of the basic techniques of performing the strength training exercises is a critical factor in the degree of success the athlete will attain from a strength training program. Without total adherence to the correct techniques, the exercises will not be performed properly; the individual cannot capitalize on his existing potential for improvement; and the athlete's susceptibility to injury while lifting is increased. All athletes should become **totally familiar** with the basic techniques for performing the basic strength exercises which are described in detail in Chapter 5. The individual who is lifting weight for the first time should devote the two or three workouts to practicing the basic movements involved in each exercise with relatively light resistance in order to gain a "working familiarity" with the proper way of performing each exercise.

MUSCLE SORENESS

In the initial stages of a properly conducted strength training program, an individual is exerting tension on infrequently used or unused muscle fibers. This tension causes waste products (specifically lactic acid and carbon dioxide) to accumulate faster than the body can either use or remove them. These waste products are believed to bring about the feeling of soreness by sensitizing local pain receptors. The best method for relieving muscle soreness and stiffness is to train for three or four successive days at a level of normal workout intensity. After this initial conditioning stage, almost all muscle soreness should disappear. Any subsequent introduction of new movements in the training program will result in the reappearance of some soreness. Temporary relief of muscle soreness can be achieved by applying heat and massage to the affected muscles in order to speed up circulation, thereby abetting the removal of any waste products.

SPOTTERS

Spotters are individuals who assist someone who is lifting weights. This assistance may be before, during, or after the completion of an exercise. A spotter has two primary responsibilities: (1) Prevent injuries to either the lifter or anyone in the adjacent vicinity, and (2) provide assistance to the lifter which facilitates the proper execution of the exercise (e.g. bring a heavy weight into the starting position for an exercise).

A spotter also aids the lifter by providing constant verbal feedback. Such feedback can stimulate the desire of the lifter to achieve an "all-out effort" by

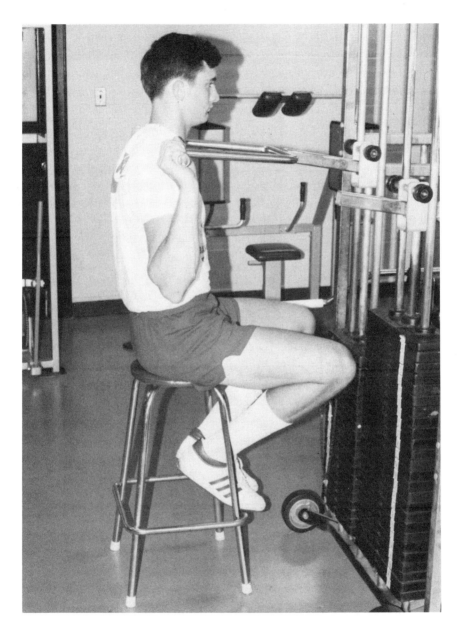

In the initial stages of a strength training program, most athletes will develop a high level of muscular soreness. Over the process of a week to 10 days, such soreness should disappear entirely. An athlete can eliminate the soreness sooner by lifting (using the same program) on three or four successive days.

discouraging him from quitting when the discomfort becomes stressful. Verbal **encouragement** also helps reinforce proper training techniques. Frequently, as the lifter becomes more fatigued, his adherence to correct form gradually decreases unless told to perform otherwise.

The guidelines for serving as a spotter are basic. During most exercises, come from beneath the weight (not over it) in order to prevent the weight from falling on the lifter. Remember that the last repetition, if performed properly, has a substantial effect on the degree of improvement achieved by the lifter. Allow the lifter to do as much work as possible on his final repetition.

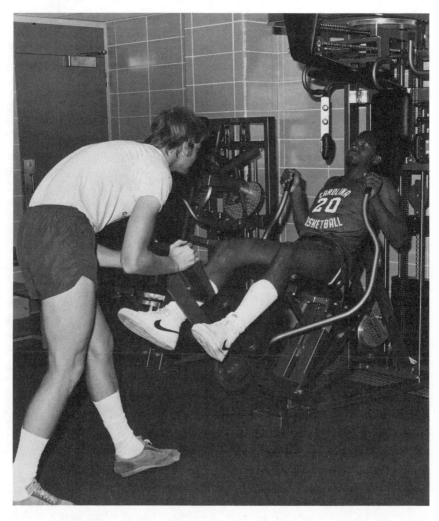

The importance of proper spotting cannot be overemphasized.

BREATHING

Breathing while engaged in strength training should be synchronized with the exercise. There is a physiological need for breathing during **each** and **every** repetition of any exercise. Adherence to the proper breathing pattern facilitates the function and efficiency of an exercise. The most consistent and efficient method that can be utilized in determining how to breathe properly is to inhale whenever the resistance is being lowered or pulled toward the body and exhale when the resistance moves away from the body (e.g., blow the weight away from the body).

The lifter should never hold his breath while training. On occasion, an inexperienced lifter holds his breath in order to "gut out" an extra repetition. More often than not, this practice results in a decrease in the efficiency of the exercise. In addition, holding one's breath while training can also produce either dizziness or unconsciousness. This condition is the result of the Valsalva Phenomenon. This phenomenon results from the buildup of inner thoracic (inner rib cage) pressure due to the great pressure or force of a weight on an individual's body who is holding his breath. This pressure, built up inside the rib cage, compresses the right side of the heart which in turn restricts the flow of blood, and consequently O_2, to the entire body. Some exercises bring on the symptoms of the Valsalva Phenomenon more readily than others (i.e., squat, seated or military press, deadlift, biceps curl, bench press).

SAFETY CONSIDERATIONS

For the individual who adheres to proper lifting techniques and utilizes a reasonable level of common sense, strength lifting is a relatively safe activity. Most injuries result from either carelessness or ignorance. The following guidelines should be followed:

- Never train with weights at a high level of intensity without having mastered the techniques involved in performing the exercise.
- Use spotters whenever necessary.
- Always make sure that plate collars for the free weights are securely tightened.
- Wear footwear in order to help cushion the blow from a falling object and to avoid stubbing the toes.
- When loading or unloading one side of a barbell, load or unload the other side evenly.
- Remember that the weight room is not a playroom. Be considerate of others.

31

RUBBER SWEAT SUITS

Perspiring is the body's primary mechanism for preventing overheating. When the temperature of the body rises, the perspiration process begins. Evaporation of perspiration cools the body surface which in turn helps control body temperature. Covering the body with a plastic or rubber sweat suit prevents the natural cooling down process of the body from taking place. The heat produced is not dissipated, and the temperature of the body continues to rise. This causes a rise in blood pressure and over-taxes the heart. Simply stated, these suits serve no practical purpose in any type of properly conducted conditioning program, strength training included.

EXERCISE ANTAGONISTS

Pairs of muscle groups which oppose each other are called antagonists (e.g., the biceps and the triceps). Practically every muscle in the body has an antagonist. To develop one muscle or group of muscles and ignore its antagonist upsets the equilibrium of the opposing muscles. As a muscle becomes stronger than its antagonist, the flexibility of the joint controlled by the affected musculature is decreased. As a result, both the joint and the involved muscles are more susceptible to injury.

Many athletes (basketball players, for example) are frequently guilty of not achieving a balance of strength in opposing muscle groups. Such individuals can be seen exercising the quadriceps by running stadium steps, riding bycicles, etc., but ignoring the hamstrings. This leads to a loss in flexibility and creates a strength imbalance in the hamstrings in relation to the quadriceps and leaves the hamstrings more susceptible to pulls and tears.

> **Most of the hamstring pulls suffered by basketball players are the result of a strength imbalance between the athletes' frontal and rear thigh muscles.**

CAROLINA

GAMECOCKS

SOUTH CAROLINA IS

TRADITION

BEAUTY

GREAT FACILITIES

SPIRIT

SOMEPLACE SPECIAL

N INSTITUTION WITH
GLORIOUS PAST,
CHALLENGING PRESENT
ND A DYNAMIC FUTURE.

EXCITEMENT

EXERCISE THROUGH A FULL RANGE OF MOVEMENT

Flexibility is defined as the capacity of a joint to move through a full range of movement. The primary factor affecting that capacity is the musculature surrounding the joint. When a skeletal joint is periodically required to go through a full range of motion, the muscles involved in the movement tend to retain their natural elasticity. When a joint is not taken through its full range of movement on a regular basis, the surrounding musculature tends to tighten up, causing it to lose some of its elasticity. As a result, the joint becomes less flexible. For the athlete, the loss of flexibility can result in both a decrease in his ability to perform and increase the chances for injury.

Contrary to superstition and unfounded myths, properly performed strength training exercises actually increase flexibility. In fact, it is impossible for an athlete who exercises through a **full range of movement** to decrease his flexibility. Adherence to correct lifting techniques enables an athlete to develop strength throughout the entire range of movement for his body's musculature (and concurrently flexibility). A coach's worry that he is developing an Arnold Schwartznegger clone is simply unfounded.

Proper strength training increases—*not decreases*—flexibility.

EMPHASIZE THE NEGATIVE PHASE OF AN EXERCISE

Two distinctive movements can be observed when an individual is performing a weight training exercise: The raising of the weight and the lowering of the weight. The raising of the weight is considered **positive work** and the lowering of the weight **negative work**. When performing positive work, the muscle is shortening (contracting). While lowering the weight, the muscle is lengthening. The muscles used to raise the weight are the same muscles used to lower the weight. For example, when lifting the weight while performing a biceps curl, the biceps muscle is shortening while doing the work. When the weight is lowered, the same muscle group is performing the work. In this instance, however, the biceps are lengthening.

The negative portion of an exercise is just as important as the positive movement. Unfortunately, negative work is often ignored by individuals engaged in weight training. Since it is easier to lower than it is to raise the same weight, the tendency is to be less conscious of form when lowering the weight. Both movements, however, should be performed as precisely as possible, perhaps placing even a greater emphasis on the lowering of the weight. It should take approximately twice as long to lower the weight (4 seconds) as it does to raise the weight (2 seconds).

NEGATIVE-ONLY EXERCISE

During an exercise performed in a negative-only manner, an athlete performs only the negative phase of the exercise. Negative-only exercising has many advantages. The greatest advantage can be observed when an individual fails and can no longer raise the weight. For example, while performing pullups, an individual fails on the 4th rep of the exercise. He cannot raise his bodyweight to properly perform a 5th rep. Most athletes stop performing the exercise at this point. Realistically, the intensity of exercise after only four reps is very low. Additional improvement could be achieved if the individual were able to continue performing the exercise for a few more reps. The resistance provided by the individual's bodyweight at that point in the exercise is too high to continue the exercise in normal fashion. The individual should then perform the exercise in a negative-only manner. He should get his chin over the bar (step on a stool or ladder) and just lower his body. While performing an exercise in negative-only fashion, 4 seconds should be taken to lower the weight.

The same concept can be used with a barbell or any conventional equipment. The spotter can help the lifter raise the weight and let the lifter lower it by himself. The total number of reps to include those performed by the lifter in a normal fashion and those performed in a negative-only fashion should not exceed 12 reps. The spotter should only record those reps on the workout card that the lifter performed in normal fashion.

NEGATIVE-ACCENTUATED EXERCISE

Negative-accentuated training is a method of exercising whereby a lifter uses two limbs to perform the positive portion of the exercise and, alternating limbs, uses one limb to perform the negative portion of the exercise. For example, an individual uses both of his legs during the positive portion of the leg extension and lowers the weight back to the starting position using only one leg. The primary advantage of negative-accentuated exercise is the great amount of resistance which can be applied to a single limb (leg or arm) during the eccentric portion of the exercise. The major disadvantages are: specific equipment is required (e.g., Nautilus, Universal, etc.), and negative-accentuated training is restricted to those exercises which involve the lifter's limbs.

CONTROL THE SPEED OF THE WEIGHT

Many athletes "throw" a weight rather than allow the muscles to lift it. They generate enough momentum so that the exercise becomes a ballistic movement. As a result, a specific muscle simply recruits fewer fibers to perform this exercise. "Throwing" the weight can be observed in many exercises, but it is particularly obvious in an exercise such as the leg extension. When raising the weight, the athlete should control the weight's speed of movement. The lifter should be able to stop the weight at any time during the "positive" movement. The weight should not be bounced or jerked during **any** part of the range of movement for **any** exercise. Throwing or jerking a weight will not improve an athlete's level of fitness or his level of "power." It simply makes him more skilled at throwing a weight. In addition, it often results in an injury to the lifter since a tremendous amount of unwarranted, explosive stress on the affected limbs of the lifter occurs during the exercise.

If a coach feels he must test his athletes, I recommend two exercises (for the upper body)—chinups and dips. Chins and dips are used because they are relatively easy to perform (little skill), easy to administer (only chin and dip bars are needed), and comparatively very safe (the risk of injury is less than for the exercises traditionally used for "testing" strength, e.g., squat, power clean, etc.).

I strongly urge every coach and athlete to keep in mind that the purpose of strength training is to **build strength, not demonstrate it!** Encourage your athletes to focus their efforts on improving themselves. The commitment for every athlete must be to be as fit as he can possibly be. Artificial goals more often than not only serve to compromise the results attained by the program.

5

ORGANIZING MUSCULAR FITNESS PROGRAMS

When organizing a program to develop muscular fitness, an athlete or a coach is confronted with seven basic variables on which the program should be based. Although there are many ways in which these variables can be manipulated to produce an increase in an athlete's level of muscular fitness, the most effective and efficient approach for achieving maximum improvement is to adhere as closely as possible to the recommendations listed under each variable.

The seven basic variables of a muscular fitness developmental program are:

1. What exercises should be performed?
2. In what order should the exercises be performed?
3. How many repetitions should be executed?
4. How much weight should be used during each exercise?
5. How many sets of each exercise should be performed?
6. How much rest should be taken between exercises?
7. How many workouts per week?

EXERCISES TO BE PERFORMED

At least one exercise should be included for each major muscle in the body (the lower back and buttocks, the legs, the torso, the arms, and the abdominals). As a general rule, the total number of exercises for the major muscle groups should not exceed ten to twelve. An additional two or three exercises for muscles specific to basektball skills (e.g., wrist flexors, forearm flexors, etc.) can be incorporated into the program to bring the total number of exercises in the program to fourteen.

The specific exercises to be performed will be dependent upon the equipment which is available. While some equipment is certainly better than other equipment, the most important factor for the athlete to remember is the fact that the key to improvement is not necessarily the tool but how he uses it. Table 5-1 presents a listing of the traditional strength training exercises for the various major muscles of the body. Chapter 6 offers a description of basic exercises using free weights, Universal Gym, and Nautilus equipment.

ORDER OF EXERCISE

Whenever possible, the athlete should exercise the potentially larger and stronger muscles of the body first. The athlete should progress from the muscles of the lower back and buttocks, to the legs, to the torso, to the arms, to the abdominals, and finish with the muscles of the neck.* The muscles of the neck are exercised last because of the fact that these muscles possess a relatively (in comparison to the rest of the body) low base level of fitness. It is simply imprudent, safety-wise, to continue strength training after the neck musculature is fatigued. The abdominals are exercised after the legs, torso, and arm muscle groups because for some exercises (e.g., the squat), the abdominals serve as a stabilizing influence. If the abdominals are fatigued before the legs, torso, and arms, when the athlete performs an exercise involving the abdominals as a stabilizer, he either compromises the level of intensity at which the exercise can be performed or the safety level of the lifter. The arms are exercised after the torso because the arms assist in exercises involving the torso (e.g., bench press, military press, etc.). The same limitations—either a decrease in intensity potential or an increase in the possibility of an injury occurring—exist.

While exercising the muscles of the torso and the arms, the athlete should attempt to alternate pushing and pulling movements whenever possible. Although in many instances an individual could follow any order of exercises and improve his level of muscular fitness, he should remember that one of his major goals, whenever possible, is to make his conditioning program as efficient as possible. **Efficiency should not be sacrificed.**

---

*Note: Personally, I do not recommend that basketball players engage in strength training exercises for the neck. If no neck exercises are to be done, the athlete should finish his workout with exercises for the abdominal muscles.

Exercise by Muscle Group and Equipment

	Free Weights	Multi Station Equipment	Variable Resistance Equipment
Buttocks/lower back	squat stiff-legged deadlift	leg press hyperextension	hip and back leg press
Quadriceps	squat	leg extension leg press	leg extension leg press
Hamstrings	squat	leg curl leg press	leg curl leg press
Calves	calf raise	toe press on leg press	calf raise on multi-exercise toe press on leg press
Latissimus dorsi	bent-over rowing bent-armed pullover stiff-armed pullover	chin-up pulldown on lat machine	pullover behind neck torso/arm chin-up on multi-exercise
Trapezius	shoulder shrug dumbbell shoulder shrug	shoulder shrug	neck and shoulder rowing torso
Deltoids	press, press behind neck upright rowing, forward raise side raise with dumbbells	seated press upright rowing	double shoulder 1. lateral raise 2. overhead press rowing torso
Pectoralis majors	bench press dumbbell flies	bench press parallel dip	double chest 1. arm cross 2. decline press parallel dip on multi-exercise
Biceps	standing curl	curl chin-up	compound curl biceps curl multi curl
Triceps	triceps extension with dumbbells	press down on lat machine	compount triceps triceps extension multi triceps
Forearms Abdominals/obliques	wrist curl sit-up side bend with dumbbells	wrist curl sit-up leg raise	wrist curl on multi-exercise sit-up on multi-exercise leg raise on mult-exercise side bend on multi-exercise
Neck	neck bridge (dangerous)	neck harness	4-way neck rotary neck neck and shoulder

Table 5-1. Basic Exercises for Strength Training

When determining the order of exercises, the exercises should be grouped by their designated body part (legs, torso, arms, abdominals, neck) and by alternate pushing and pulling movements for the torso and arm muscles.

Legs — buttocks, quadriceps, hamstrings, calves.
Torso — deltoids, lats, pectorals, lower back, trapezius.
Arms — triceps, biceps, forearms.
Abdomen — obliques, rectus abdominis, transverse abdominis.
Neck — flexors, extensors.

HOW MANY REPETITIONS?

The number of repetitions which each exercise should be performed is based upon the athlete's subjective evaluation of the validity of two schools of thought. The traditional philosophy recommends that the number of repetitions to be performed is dependent upon the goals of the program. If the athlete wants to develop strength, he should perform sets of 5 to 8 repetitions. If he desires to build muscular endurance, he should perform sets of 9-15 repetitions. The primary proponents of this philosophy are free weight enthusiasts and Universal Gym users.

A contrasting theory which has been developed in the last ten years is the philosophy which recommends that regardless of your personal muscular fitness developmental objectives, one set of 8-12 repetitions should be performed. Although Nautilus Sports/Medical Industries equipment proponents are the major commercial advocates of this approach, many individuals, including numerous coaches, exercise physiologists, physicians, and trainers, feel that this protocol is the best approach **regardless** of the type of equipment used.

Regardless of a coach's personal philosophy regarding the relative merits of the two contrasting techniques, he should categorically reject the mentality that insinuates that "more is better." There is obviously a point of diminishing returns regarding the expenditure of effort. The goal of all conditioning programs should be to develop fitness in an efficient and effective manner as possible—not engage in lengthy workouts merely for the sake of working out.

HOW MUCH WEIGHT?

The athlete should initially learn how to properly perform each exercise before progressing to a weight which places a substantial demand on him. Once the correct techniques have been learned, the athlete, through trial and error, should select a weight that will cause him to reach the point of muscular failure somewhere between his arbitrarily predetermined number of repetitions. The point of muscular failure has been reached when the athlete can no longer raise the weight in good form through the muscles' full range of movement.

If the athlete fails before he reaches the minimal number of the predetermined lower limit of repetitions, the weight is too heavy. If he can properly perform more than the upper limit of repetitions, the weight is too light and more weight should be added. The "overload principle" should be observed if the athlete is to increase his level of muscular fitness. The overload principle simply states that the athlete should, whenever possible within his personal limits and within the recommended guidelines for developing muscular fitness, increase the amount of weight used or the number of repetitions performed during the execution of each exercise. Once the predetermined number of maximum repetitions is reached, the athlete should have a training partner assist him to perform two or three additional repetitions in order to achieve additional gains in strength and endurance.

Regardless of what an individual's intuition may tell him, more is *not* definitely always better—particularly in the weight room.

HOW MANY SETS?

A set involves the number of repetitions executed each time an exercise is performed. Similar to the controversy surrounding the question of how many repetitions should be performed, two major approaches exist concerning the number of sets which should be performed. The traditional philosophy states that three sets should be performed. The contrasting theory (developed through the auspices and research efforts of Nautilus Sports/Medical Industries) recommends that only a single set be performed. The reasoning basis for this theory holds that one "properly performed" set will stimulate maximum gains in muscular strength and mass. If an athlete properly performs one set, he will certainly not want to perform a second set; and if he did perform additional exercise, it could eventually become counterproductive. If a second set is performed, it is obvious that the first set was not properly performed. Advocates of this philosophy argue that too many athletes associate gains in strength with the number of sets performed, totally disregarding that it is how each exercise is performed that stimulates strength gains. When multiple sets are performed, some athletes can be observed "holding back" and pacing themselves for the last set to be executed. Although this method of training can produce significant gains, the time spent is prolonged and unnecessary.

Regardless of the philosophy which is adopted, one of an athlete's primary objectives should be to organize a workout that will produce the maximum level improvement in the most efficient amount of time. The two hour weight training workout is neither needed nor productive. A three-set workout typically requires only approximately 1 hour to complete, while a 1-set workout takes less than 30 minutes.

> One of the primary objectives of a strength training program should be to achieve the maximum level of improvement possible, in the least amount of time and in the safest manner feasible.

HOW MUCH REST BETWEEN EXERCISES?

In general, an athlete should move from one exercise to the next, allowing only a minimal time to rest between exercises. If a "typical" strength training workout were to be observed, in many instances, a coach would find that most athletes spend more time resting between exercises than they actually spend lifting weights. A reasonable rest period between exercises is somewhere between 30 seconds and 1 minute. Any greater rest period can lead to a time-consuming, prolonged training session. In addition, an athlete can develop his level of aerobic fitness, concurrently with his efforts to increase his level of muscular fitness, by moving from one exercise to the next in a non-stop fashion. This method of training consumes less time and places a substantial demand on his cardiovascular system. As a result, his level of aerobic fitness is improved.

HOW MANY WORKOUTS PER WEEK?

If a muscle is not exercised every 48-72 hours, it will begin to atrophy (grow weaker and smaller). Also, a muscle when overloaded, needs at least 48 hours to fully recover. During his off-season, an athlete should train three times per week on alternate days. During the in-season period, an athlete should work out at least once, and preferably twice, a week to maintain his muscular fitness level. Ideally, the in-season workouts should include at least one high intensity workout and one less vigorous workout. If more than two workouts are conducted, two of the sessions should be of relatively high intensity. In this instance, the less intense workout should be performed in between the two high intensity workouts.

6
MUSCULAR FITNESS EXERCISES AND PROGRAMS

As I indicated in earlier chapters, it is not so much the tool, but the way an athlete uses a tool, which will enable him to develop muscular fitness. Quite frankly,, there are numerous tools and techniques for developing strength. Obviously, some are more effective and therefore more popular than others. From the equipment which is available to them, coaches and athletes should select those methods which they feel work best for them.

The purpose of this chapter is to present an overview description of how to perform the various strength training exercises using free weights, Universal Gym, and Nautilus equipment. The descriptions are grouped by equipment type and are listed in order of largest muscles to smallest for each type of equipment. The muscle or muscle group developed by that exercise, information on how to perform the exercise, and important points to remember when doing the exercise are also presented. Figures 6-1 and 6-2 illustrate the major muscles of the body. Sample workout programs using each of the three basic types of equipment are prescribed in Table 6-1.

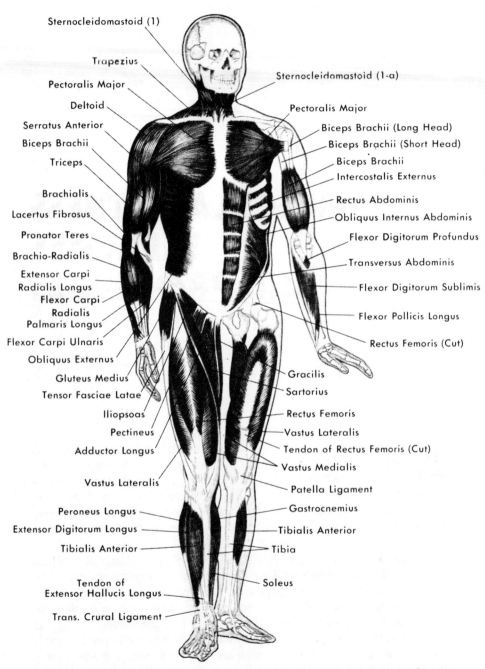

Sternocleidomastoid (1)

Trapezius

Pectoralis Major

Deltoid

Serratus Anterior

Biceps Brachii

Triceps

Brachialis

Lacertus Fibrosus

Pronator Teres

Brachio-Radialis

Extensor Carpi
Radialis Longus
Flexor Carpi
Radialis
Palmaris Longus

Flexor Carpi Ulnaris

Obliquus Externus

Gluteus Medius

Tensor Fasciae Latae

Iliopsoas

Pectineus

Adductor Longus

Vastus Lateralis

Peroneus Longus

Extensor Digitorum Longus

Tibialis Anterior

Tendon of
Extensor Hallucis Longus

Trans. Crural Ligament

Sternocleidomastoid (1-a)

Pectoralis Major

Biceps Brachii (Long Head)

Biceps Brachii (Short Head)

Biceps Brachii

Intercostalis Externus

Rectus Abdominis

Obliquus Internus Abdominis

Flexor Digitorum Profundus

Transversus Abdominis

Flexor Digitorum Sublimis

Flexor Pollicis Longus

Rectus Femoris (Cut)

Gracilis

Sartorius

Rectus Femoris

Vastus Lateralis

Tendon of Rectus Femoris (Cut)

Vastus Medialis

Patella Ligament

Gastrocnemius

Tibialis Anterior

Tibia

Soleus

Figure 6-1. Muscles of the body: anterior view (Reprinted by permission of Cramer Products Inc.)

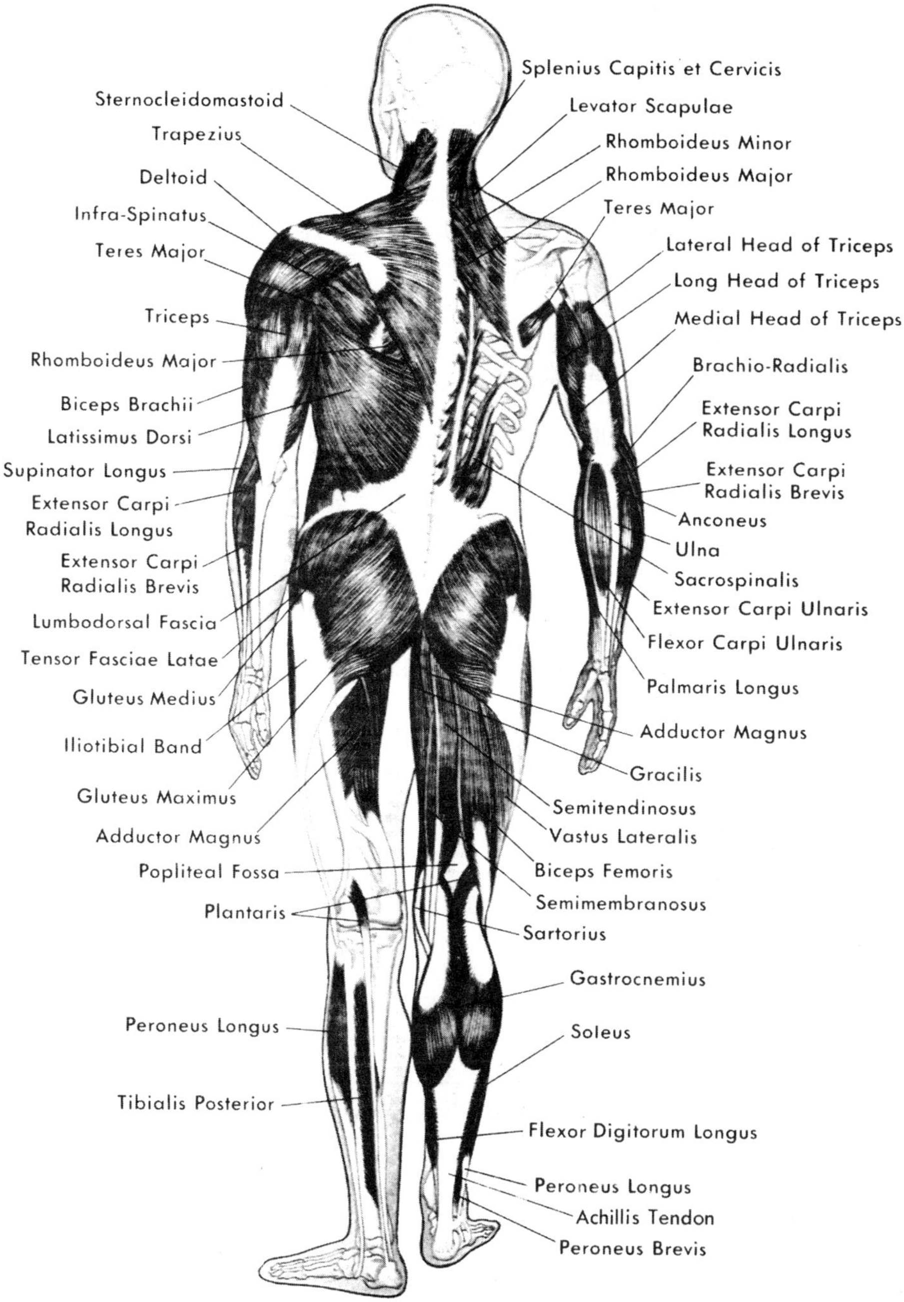

Figure 6-2. Muscles of the body: posterior view. (Reprinted by permission of Cramer Products Inc.)

Muscular Fitness Exercises and Programs

Table 6-1. Sample strength training workout programs.

SAMPLE FREE WEIGHT WORKOUT

- Dead Lift
- Squat
- Leg Curl with Partner
- Leg Extension with Partner
- Foot Flexion with Partner
- Bench Press
- Chin Ups
- Seated Press
- Side Lateral Raise
- Shoulder Shrugs
- Bicep Curls
- Tricep Extension
- Wrist Curls
- Sit-Ups

SAMPLE UNIVERSAL GYM WORKOUT

- Leg Press
- Leg Curl
- Leg Extension
- Heel Raise
- Foot Flexion
- Bench Press
- Seated Press
- Lat Pulldown
- Shoulder Shrug
- Upright Row
- Bicep Curl
- Tricep Extension
- Wrist Curl
- Sit-Ups

SAMPLE NAUTILUS WORKOUT

- Hip and Back
- Leg Extension
- Leg Press
- Leg Curl
- Abduction-Adduction
- Arm Cross
- Decline Press
- Super Pullover
- Torso Arm Pulldown
- Side Lateral Raise
- Overhead Press
- Bicep Curl (alternate)
- Tricep Extension (alternate)
- Abdominal Curl

FREE WEIGHT EXERCISES

"Free weight" equipment includes barbells, dumbbells, or any other device that allows movement through an extensive range of motion, yet is unattached to a stabilized apparatus. The advantages of "free weights" are that they are inexpensive, they are present in almost every school that has a gymnasium, and they require the athlete to maintain control and balance throughout the exercise.

A list of the major exercises which can be performed using free weights includes:

1. Dead Lift		11. Bent Over Rowing
2. Parallel Squat		12. Bent Over Flys
3. Leg Curl		13. Seated Press Behind Neck
4. Leg Extension		14. Side Lateral Raise
5. Heel Raise		15. Upright Row
6. Foot Flexion		16. Shoulder Shrug
7. Bench Press		17. Bicep Curl
8. Bent Arm Flys		18. French Curl
9. Parallel Dips		19. Wrist Curls
10. Chin Up		20. Sit Ups
	21. Hip Extension	

DEAD LIFT

Equipment Used: Barbell

Major Muscles Involved: Spinal erectors, gluteus maximus, quadriceps

Description of Exercise:

- Stand with your feet slightly greater than shoulder width.
- Squat and grip bar with an underhand grip on your non-dominant hand and an overhand grip on your dominant hand.
- Keep your elbows outside of your knees and your head up.
- Pull bar while straightening both your legs and back until you are standing straight with your shoulders back.
- Pause, slowly recover to the starting position and repeat.

Important Points:

- Keep your back straight and lift with your legs.
- Keep the bar close to your shins throughout the exercise.
- Roll your shoulders back at the completion of the positive movement.

Dead lift: starting position

Dead lift: pause position

PARALLEL SQUAT

Equipment Used: Barbell

Major Muscles Involved: Gluteus maximum, quadriceps

Description of Exercise:
- Place the barbell on back of your shoulders and assume a comfortable grip.
- Spread your feet slightly greater than shoulder width and point your toes slightly outward.
- Squat slowly downward in a knee bend until the tops of your thighs are parallel with the floor.
- Pause, recover to the starting position and repeat.

Important Points:
- Keep your head up and your back straight throughout the movement.
- Do not bounce at the bottom of the movement.
- Heel supports such as 2-1/2 lb. plates may be used until your ankle flexibility increases to a sufficiently high level.
- Since this exercise begins with the negative movement, always use spotters.

Parallel squat: starting position

Parallel squat: pause position

LEG CURL

Equipment Used: No equipment necessary

Major Muscles Involved: Hamstrings

Description of Exercise:
- Lie flat on ground with both of your legs extended.
- Your partner should place his hands behind your left heel.
- While your partner applies resistance, curl your foot as high as possible (at least perpendicular).
- Pause, slowly recover to the starting position and repeat.
- When your left leg is exhausted, perform the same exercise with your right leg.

Important Points:
- Your partner should apply enough resistance so that a maximum effort takes two seconds for the positive movement and four seconds for the negative.
- Keep your body flat on ground.

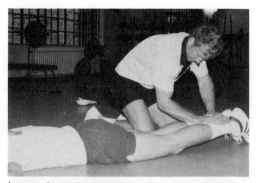

Leg curl: starting position

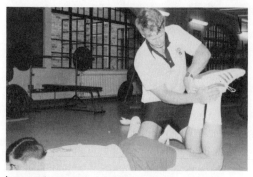

Leg curl: pause position

LEG EXTENSION

Equipment Used: No equipment necessary

Major Muscles Involved: Quadriceps

Description of Exercise:

- Lie flat on ground with your left leg flexed as far as possible.
- Your partner should place his hands in front of your left foot.
- While your partner applies resistance, push your foot back and downward until your leg is extended.
- Pause, slowly recover to the starting position and repeat.
- When your left leg is exhausted, perform the same exercise with your right leg.

Important Points:

- Your partner should apply enough resistance so that a maximum effort takes two seconds for the positive movement and four seconds for the negative.
- Do not raise your knee off of the ground.

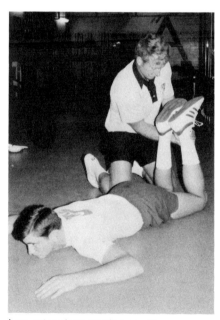
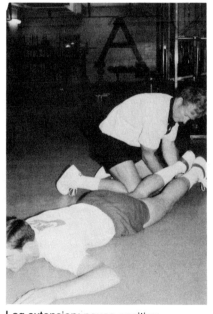

Leg extension: starting position   Leg extension: pause position

HEEL RAISE

Equipment Used: Barbell

Major Muscles Involved: Calves

Description of Exercise:
- Place the barbell across your shoulders and assume a comfortable grip with your hands.
- Spread your feet shoulder width apart and place the balls of your feet on a block of wood.
- Elevate your heels as high as possible.
- Pause, slowly recover to the starting position and repeat.

Important Points:
- Keep your back straight and your head up.
- Do not rest when your heels touch the ground.

Heel raise: starting position   Heel raise: pause position

FOOT FLEXION

Equipment Used: Towel

Major Muscles Involved: Tibialis anterior

Description of Exercise:

- Sit on ground with both of your legs extended and your feet flexed.
- Your partner should loop a towel over the toes on your right foot.
- Your partner should apply enough resistance so that a maximum effort takes two seconds for the positive movement and four seconds for the negative.
- Pause, slowly recover to the starting position and repeat.
- When your right leg is exhausted, repeat the exercise with your left leg.

Important Points:

- Place towel high on your toes for maximum leverage.
- Keep your knee straight throughout the movement.

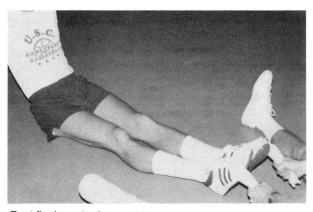

Foot flexion: starting position

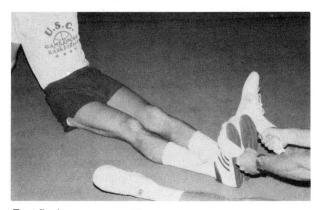

Foot flexion: pause position

BENCH PRESS

Equipment Used: Barbell

Major Muscles Involved: Pectorals, deltoids, triceps

Description of Exercise:

- Lie flat on a bench with the back of your shoulders and your buttocks flat on the bench.
- Bend your knees and place your feet flat on floor.
- Grip the bar slightly wider than shoulder width.
- Lower the bar to the center of your chest and pause.
- Push your arms upward until your elbows are extended, and repeat.

Important Points:

- Do not raise your buttocks off of bench.
- Do not bounce the weight off of chest.
- Exhale while raising the weight.
- When using near maximum weight, utilize spotters.

Bench press: starting position

Bench press: pause position

BENT ARM FLYS

Equipment Used: Dumbbells

Major Muscles Involved: Pectorals, deltoids

Description of Exercise:
- Lie flat on a bench with your knees bent and your feet flat on floor.
- Hold the dumbbells over your chest with your elbows slightly bent, your palms facing inward and dumbbells touching each other.
- Slowly lower the dumbbells outward and downward, keeping your elbows bent until a maximum stretch is achieved.
- Pause, recover to the starting position and repeat.

Important Points:
- Keep your elbows bent throughout the exercise.
- Raise and lower your arms as if hugging a barrel.

Bent arm flys: starting position

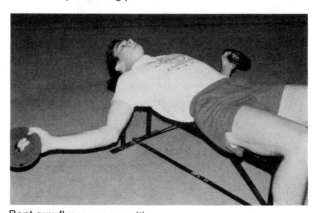

Bent arm flys: pause position

PARALLEL DIPS

Equipment Used: Parallel Bars

Major Muscles Involved: Pectorals, deltoids, triceps

Description of Exercise:

- Grip the parallel bars with your palms facing inward.
- Suspend the weight with your elbows slightly bent and your knees flexed.
- Slowly lower your body by bending your elbows as far as possible.
- Pause, recover to the starting position and repeat.

Important Points:

- Do not swing your body during exercise.
- Pause at the bottom of the movement.

Parallel dips: starting position   Parallel dips: pause position

CHIN-UPS

Equipment Used: Any sturdy bar

Major Muscles Involved: Latissimus dorsi, biceps

Description of Exercise:
- Grip the bar with an underhand grip; your hands should be shoulder width apart.
- Hang from the bar with your elbows straight.
- Raise your body upward until your chin is above the bar.
- Pause, slowly recover to the starting position and repeat.

Important Points:
- Do not allow your body to swing during the exercise.
- Allow your elbow to extend completely at the bottom of the movement.

Chin-ups: starting position   Chin-ups: pause position

BENT OVER ROWING

Equipment Used: Barbell

Major Muscles Involved: Latissimus dorsi, biceps.

Description of Exercise:

- Stand with your feet shoulder width apart and your knees slightly bent.
- Bend forward at the waist until your torso is parallel with the floor.
- Grip the bar with an overhand grip; your hands held greater than shoulder width apart.
- Raise the bar to the center of your chest.
- Pause, slowly lower the resistance to the starting position and repeat.

Important Points:

- Keep your head up and your back straight.
- Keep your back parallel with the floor.

Bent over rowing: starting position

Bent over rowing: pause position

BENT OVER FLYS

Equipment Used: Dumbbells

Major Muscles Involved: Latissimus dorsi, rhomboids.

Description of Exercise:
- Stand with your feet shoulder width apart and your knees slightly bent.
- Bend forward at your waist until your torso is parallel with the floor.
- Grip the dumbbells with your palms facing inward, your arms straight, and the dumbbells touching each other.
- Raise your arms laterally as high as possible.
- Pause, slowly recover to the starting position and repeat.

Important Points:
- Keep your head up and your back straight.
- Keep your back parallel to the floor throughout the exercise.

Bent over fly:
starting position

Bent over fly: pause position

PRESS BEHIND NECK

Equipment Used: Barbell

Major Muscles Involved: Deltoids, triceps

Description of Exercise:
- Sit on a bench with your feet flat on the floor.
- Grip the barbell with your hands greater than shoulder width distance apart and place the barbell on the back of your shoulders.
- Extend your arms overhead until your elbows are straight.
- Pause, slowly recover to the starting position and repeat.

Important Points:
- Lower the bar slowly; do not bounce it off of your neck.
  Do not arch your back because it will place considerable stress on your lower back.

Press behind neck: starting position

Press behind neck: pause position

UPRIGHT ROW

Equipment Used: Barbell

Major Muscles Involved: Deltoids, trapezius

Description of Exercise:

- Stand with your feet shoulder width apart and your arms extended downward.
- Grip the bar with an overhand grip, your hands less than shoulder width apart.
- Pull the bar upward without bending your torso until the bar touches your chin.
- Pause, slowly recover to the starting position and repeat.

Important Points:

- Stand straight with your head up throughout the exercise.
- Pull the bar all the way to your chin.

Upright row: starting position

Upright row: pause position

LATERAL RAISE

Equipment Used: Dumbbells

Major Muscles Involved: Deltoids

Description of Exercise:
- Stand with your feet shoulder width apart and your arms extended downward.
- Face your palms inward while holding the dumbbells at your side.
- Raise the dumbbells laterally until your arms are parallel with the floor.
- Pause, slowly recover to the starting position.

Important Points:
- Stand as straight as possible.
- Do not raise the weights above shoulder level in order to prevent other muscles from becoming involved.

Lateral raise:
starting position

Lateral raise: pause position

SHOULDER SHRUG

Equipment Used: Barbell

Major Muscles Involved: Trapezius

Description of Exercise:

- Stand with your feet shoulder width apart and your arms extended downward.
- Grip the bar with an overhand grip, your hands shoulder width apart.
- Keep your arms straight and raise your shoulders as high as possible.
- Pause, slowly recover to the starting position and repeat.

Important Points:

- Stand straight throughout the exercise.
- Allow your shoulders to drop as far as possible at the bottom of the movement.

Shoulder shrug: starting position

Shoulder shrug: pause position

BICEP CURL

Equipment Used: Barbell or easy curl bar

Major Muscles Involved: Biceps

Description of Exercise:
- Stand with your feet less than shoulder width apart and your arms extended downward.
- Grip the bar with an underhand grip, your hands just outside of your hips apart.
- Keep your elbows back and curl the bar as high as possible.
- Pause, slowly recover to the starting position and repeat.

Important Points:
- Keep your back straight; do not lean back.
- Keep your elbows back throughout the exercise.

Bicep curl: starting position

Bicep curl: pause position

FRENCH CURL

Equipment Used: Barbell

Major Muscles Involved: Triceps

Description of Exercise:

- Lie flat on a bench with your knees bent and your feet flat on the floor.
- Grip the bar with an overhand grip, your hands less than shoulder width apart.
- Your upper arms should be perpendicular to the floor with the bar just above your forehead.
- Extend your arms upward until your elbows are straight.
- Pause, slowly recover to the starting position.

Important Points:

- Keep your upper arms perpendicular to the bench throughout the exercise.
- Keep your elbows a shoulder width distance apart throughout the exercise.

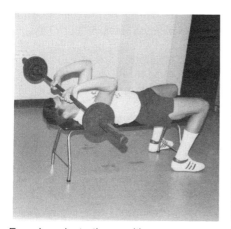

French curl: starting position   French curl: pause position

WRIST CURL

Equipment Used: Barbell

Muscles Involved: Forearm flexors

Description of Exercise:
- Sit on the ond of a bench with your knees bent and your feet flat on the floor.
- Place your forearms firmly against your thighs.
- Grip the bar with an underhand grip and allow the bar to roll to the end of your finger tips.
- Curl your fingers upward and flex your wrists.
- Pause, slowly recover to the starting position and repeat.

Important Points:
- Keep your forearms in contact with your thighs throughout the exercise.
- Allow your fingers to extend downward as far as possible at the bottom of movement.

Wrist curl: starting position

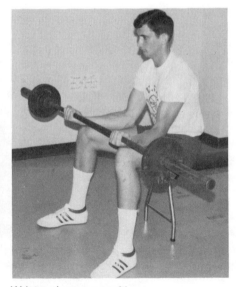
Wrist curl: pause position

REVERSE WRIST CURL

Equipment Used: Barbell

Major Muscles Involved: Forearm extensors

Description of Exercise:

- Sit on the end of the bench with your knees bent and your feet flat on the floor.
- Place your forearms firmly against your thighs.
- Grip the bar with an overhand grip and allow your wrists to bend downward.
- Curl your wrists upward and backward as far as possible.
- Pause, slowly recover to the starting position and repeat.

Important Points:

- Keep your forearms in contact with your thighs throughout the exercise.
- Keep your wrists just over the ends of your knees.

Reverse wrist curl: starting position   Reverse wrist curl: pause position

SIT-UP

Equipment Used: Cushions

Major Muscles Involved: Abdominals

Description of Exercise:
- Sit on the floor with cushions placed under your buttocks.
- Bend your knees and place your feet flat on the floor.
- Your partner should hold your feet in place.
- Lace your fingers behind your head and assume a position where your torso is approximately one inch from the floor.
- Curl your torso upward to a point just short of vertical (perpendicular).
- Pause, slowly recover to the starting position and repeat.

Important Points:
- You pause on the raising phase at a point just short of vertical or your abdominals will be allowed to relax.
- When you can perform more than 15 repetitions, hold a 5-10 pound plate behind your head while performing the sit-ups.

Sit-up: starting position

Sit-up: pause position

HIP EXTENSION*

Equipment Used: Refer to description on page 69.

Major Muscles Involved: Lower back and gluteus maximus

Description of Exercise: Refer to description on page 69.

*Editor's note: As an outgrowth of his strength studies conducted at West Point, Dr. James A. Peterson developed the hip extension exercise for strengthening the lower back and buttocks. Unlike most of the machines which purport to accomplish the same goal, the hip extension (as explained on page 69) is highly effective for improving vertical jumping ability, safe, and costs almost nothing for the equipment involved. Used with permission.

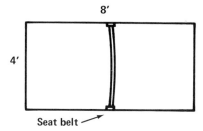

Side view of the athlete, strapped-in.

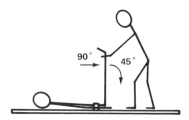

Partner holds the back of the athlete's ankles.

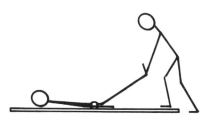

Keeping his knees locked, the athlete moves his legs downward to the 45° position.

- A 4'x8' piece of plywood and an automobile seat belt are required.
- Attach the (velcro) seat belt to the middle of the plywood.
- Athlete lies flat on his back on the plywood and attaches the seat belt across his abdomen.
- Training partner raises both legs of the athlete to a 90° angle or as far as they can go up to 90° maximum.
- The athlete should keep his knees locked throughout the exercise and his arms to the side.
- On the command "go", the athlete moves his legs in a downward motion against a force being exerted by his training partner. The athlete's knees should be locked at all times.
- The training partner should control the downward movement of the athlete's legs and allow the legs to move in a steady, smooth pattern. It should take about 4 seconds for the athlete to move his legs from the 90° position to about a 45° position (approximately the knee level of the training partner). Once he reaches 45°, the training partner should command "stop"; the athlete on his own should raise his legs back to the 90°point; and the exercise repeated.
- If he keeps his legs locked, the muscles used by the athlete to move his legs in a downward motion are the lower back and the buttock muscles.

UNIVERSAL GYM EXERCISES

A Universal Gym (or any other multi-station apparatus, e.g., Paramount, Pro Gym, etc.) can be found in nearly every school (both colleges and high schools) in the country. These machines are popular because they are easy to use, do not require spotters, have built-in safety features, can accommodate several athletes at the same time, and are not overly expensive.

A list of the major exercises that can be performed using the Universal Gym includes:

1. Leg Press
2. Leg Curl
3. Leg Extension
4. Heel Raise
5. Foot Flexion
6. Bench Press
7. Rowing
8. Seated Press
9. Lat Pulldown
10. Shoulder Shrug
11. Upright Row
12. Bicep Curl
13. Tricep Extension
14. Wrist Curl/Reverse Wrist Curl
15. Sit Ups/Leg Raises

LEG PRESS

Equipment Used: Leg press station

Major Muscles Involved: Gluteus maximus, quadriceps

Description of Exercise:
- Sit with your shoulders against the seat back and the balls of your feet centered on the foot pads.
- Adjust the seat so that your knee joints are less than a 90° angle.
- Loosely grip the handles.
- Straighten both legs but do not "lock out" to prevent your thigh muscles from relaxing.
- Pause, slowly recover to the starting position and repeat.

Important Points:
- Do not grip the handles tightly.
- Do not bounce the weight stack at the bottom of the movement.

Leg press: starting position

Leg press: pause position

LEG CURL

Equipment Used: Leg curl station

Major Muscles Involved: Hamstrings

Description of Exercise:

- Lie face down on the bench.
- Place the back of your ankles under roller pads with your kneecaps just off of the end of the bench.
- Curl your legs upward as far as possible.
- Pause, slowly recover to the starting position and repeat.

Important Points:

- Your feet should be in a flexed position with your toes pointing towards your knees.
- Your feet should be at least perpendicular in the contracted position.

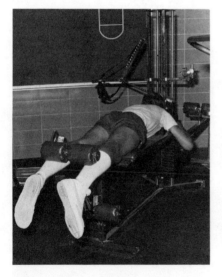

Leg curl: starting position

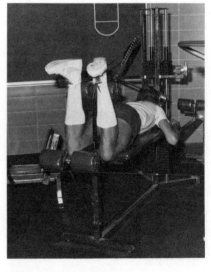

Leg curl: pause position

LEG EXTENSION

Equipment Used: Leg extension station

Major Muscles Involved: Quadriceps

Description of Exercise:

- In a seated position, place both your feet behind the roller pads with the back of your knees against the front of the seat.
- Keep your hand and shoulders in a vertical position throughout the exercise.
- Raise your feet until both your legs are straight.
- Pause, slowly recover to the starting position and repeat.

Important Points:

- Grip the side of the bench loosely with your hands.
- Relax your hands, neck, and face muscles during the exercise.

Leg extension: starting position

Leg extension: pause position

HEEL RAISE

Equipment Used: Seated press station

Major Muscles Involved: Calves

Description of Exercise:
- Stand facing the weight stack.
- Grip the handles with an overhand grip and raise the weights to a shoulder level height.
- Place the balls of your feet on a block of wood.
- Elevate your heels as high as possible.
- Pause, slowly recover to the starting position and repeat.

Important Points:
- Do not let your heels touch the ground.
- Do not bend your knees.

Heel raise: starting position   Heel raise: pause position

FOOT FLEXION

Equipment Used: Leg curl station

Major Muscles Involved: Tibialis anterior

Description of Exercise:
- In a seated position, place three cushions under your calves.
- Place your toes under the roller pads.
- Keep your torso in a vertical position and loosely grip the sides of the bench.
- Curl your toes back towards your knees as far as possible.
- Pause, slowly recover to the starting position and repeat.

Important Points:
- Allow your feet to extend completely on the negative movement.
- Cushions may be added or subtracted for comfort.

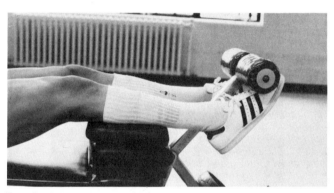

Foot flexion: starting position

Foot flexion: pause position

BENCH PRESS

Equipment Used: Bench press station

Major Muscles Involved: Pectorals, deltoids, triceps

Description of Exercise:

- Lie flat on a bench with your knees bent and your feet flat on the floor.
- Adjust the bench so that the handles are aligned with the center of your chest.
- Grip the handles with an overhand grip, hands slightly wider than shoulder width apart.
- Straighten your arms until your elbows are fully extended.
- Pause, slowly recover to the starting position and repeat.

Important Points:

- A block of wood may be placed under the head of the bench for a greater range of movement.
- Do not arch your back.
- Do not bounce the weight stack at the bottom.
- Exhale while raising the weight.

Bench press: starting position

Bench press: pause position

ROWING

Equipment Used: Bicep curl station

Major Muscles Involved: Latissimus dorsi, rhomboids, biceps

Description of Exercise:
- Sit on the floor with your legs extended and your torso in a vertical position.
- Grip handles with an overhand grip, hands shoulder width apart.
- Pull the bar as close to center of your chest as possible.
- Pause, slowly recover to the starting position and repeat.

Important Point:
- If the weight stack is touching bottom in the extended position, place a 45 pound plate between the base of the machine and your feet.

Rowing: starting position   Rowing: pause position

SEATED PRESS

Equipment Used: Seated press station

Major Muscles Involved: Deltoids, triceps

Description of Exercise:
- Sit on a stool facing away from the weight stack.
- Adjust the seat so that the handles are directly above your shoulders
- Grip the handles with an overhand grip, slightly wider than shoulder width apart.
- Place your feet on the bottom rung of the stool.
- Straighten your arms overhead until your elbows are completely extended.
- Pause, slowly recover to the starting position and repeat.

Important Points:
- If a strain is placed on your lower back in the extended position, the seat may be too far from the weight stack.
- Do not arch your back.

Seated press: starting position   Seated press: pause position

LAT PULLDOWN

Equipment Used: Lat pulldown station

Major Muscles Involved: Latissimus dorsi, biceps

Description of Exercise:

- Assume a kneeling position facing the weight stack.
- Grip the curved handles on the bar.
- Pull the bar downward and touch the base of your neck.
- Pause, slowly recover to the starting position and repeat.

Important Points:

- If you prefer, you can perform this exercise while in a sitting position.
- A closer grip may be used to place more emphasis on your biceps.

Lat pulldown: starting position   Lat pulldown: pause position

SHOULDER SHRUG

Equipment Used: Bench press station

Major Muscles Involved: Trapezius

Description of Exercise:
- Stand between the bench press handles and face the weight stack.
- Hold the inside of the handles with an overhand grip.
- Keep your arms straight and raise your shoulders upward as high as possible.
- Pause, slowly recover to the starting position and repeat.

Important Points:
- Keep your body perfectly straight.
- Allow your arms to drop as far as possible on the negative movement without bending your back.

Shoulder shrug: starting position   Shoulder shrug: pause position

UPRIGHT ROW

Equipment Used: Bicep curl station

Major Muscles Involved: Trapezius, deltoids, biceps

Description of Exercise:

- Stand facing the bicep curl station and grip the handles with an overhand grip, hands less than shoulder width apart.
- Pull the bar upward until the bar touches the bottom side of your chin.
- Pause, slowly recover to the starting position and repeat.

Important Points:

- Stand straight with your head up throughout the exercise.
- Keep your elbows pointed to the outside.
- Pull the bar all the way to your chin.

Upright row: starting position   Upright row: pause position

BICEP CURL

Equipment Used: Bicep curl station

Muscles Involved: Biceps

Description of Exercise:
- Stand with your arms extended downward and face the bicep curl station.
- Grip the bar shoulder width apart using an underhand grip.
- Curl the bar forward and upward, keeping your elbows back until the bar touches the base of your neck.
- Pause, slowly recover to the starting position and repeat.

Important Points:
- Do not allow your elbows to come forward.
- Do not lean back during the exercise.

Bicep curl: starting position

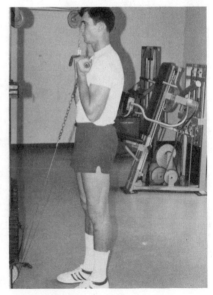

Bicep curl: pause position

TRICEP EXTENSION

Equipment Used: Lat pulldown station

Major Muscles Involved: Triceps

Description of Exercise:
- Stand facing the pulldown station with your feet shoulder width apart.
- Grip the bar with an overhand grip less than shoulder width apart.
- Pull the bar downward until your elbows are at your sides.
- Push your hands downward until your arms are extended.
- Pause, slowly recover to the starting position and repeat.

Important Points:
- Your elbows must be kept at your sides.
- Wrapping your thumbs over the bar makes it easier to stabilize your wrists.
- For greater range of movement, wrap a towel around the cable junction of the bar, grip both sides of the towel and extend the towel downward.

Tricep extension: starting position   Tricep extension: pause position

WRIST CURL

Equipment Used: Bicep curl station

Major Muscles Involved: Forearm flexors

Description of Exercise:
- Sit on the end of an exercise bench with your forearms resting on your knees.
- Grasp the handles of the curl station with an underhand grip and raise the handles until the weight stack is lifted.
- Allow the handles to rest on your finger tips.
- Curl the bar up toward your elbows as far as possible.
- Pause, slowly recover to the starting position and repeat.

Important Points:
- Keep your forearms flat on your thighs throughout the exercise.
- Your wrists should be just over end of your knees.

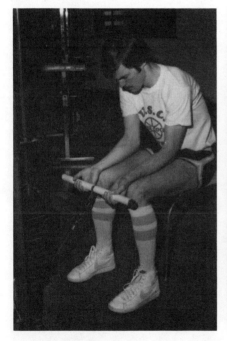

Wrist curl: starting position   Wrist curl: pause position

REVERSE WRIST CURL

Equipment Used: Bicep curl station

Major Muscles Involved: Forearm extensors

Description of Exercise:

- Sit on the end of an exercise bench with your forearms resting on your knees.
- Grasp the handles with an overhand grip.
- Curl the bar up toward your elbows as far as possible.
- Pause, slowly recover to the starting position and repeat.

Important Points:

- Keep your forearms flat on your thighs throughout the exercise.
- Your wrists should be just over end of your knees.

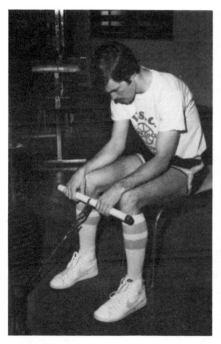

Reverse wrist curl: starting position   Reverse wrist curl: pause position

SIT-UPS

Equipment Used: Incline board

Major Muscles Involved: Abdominals, hip flexors

Description of Exercise:
- Lie face up on an incline board with your knees bent.
- Hook your feet under the roller pads and interlace your fingers behind your head.
- Curl your torso upward and forward to a point just short of being perpendicular with the floor.
- Pause, slowly recover to the starting position and repeat.

Important Points:
- Keep your knees bent.
- When more than 15 repetitions can be performed, raise the end of bench one level higher.
- Lower your torso slowly during the negative movement.
- Begin the next repetition immediately.

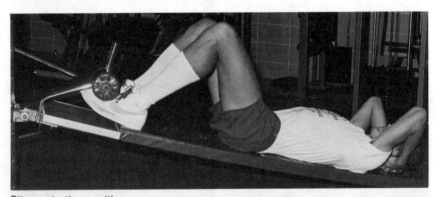

Sit-up: starting position

Sit-up: pause position

LEG RAISES

Equipment Used: Incline board

Major Muscles Involved: Abdominals, hip flexors

Description of Exercise:

- Lie face up on incline board with your knees and elbows slightly bent.
- Grip the post at the top of the board.
- Raise your legs upward and forward until your knees are perpendicular with the floor.
- Pause, slowly recover to the starting position and repeat.

Important Points:

- When more than 15 repetitions can be performed, move the board one level higher.
- Lower your legs slowly during the negative movement.

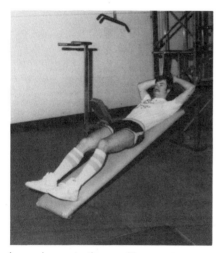

Leg raises: starting position

Leg raises: pause position

NAUTILUS EXERCISES

Nautilus equipment, despite the fact that it has been on the market only in the last decade or so and is relatively expensive (comparatively), is highly popular and widely used by coaches and athletes. The major advantages of Nautilus equipment are: the machines provide full range exercise; each machine isolates a specific muscle group; the variable resistance capability of Nautilus enables each muscle to be fully exhausted in only one set; and a high intensity workout can be completed by an athlete in approximately 20-30 minutes.

In addition to the basic techniques and principles for developing muscular fitness presented in Chapters 4 and 5, the following guidelines are recommended for those who use Nautilus equipment:

- On machines where seat adjustment and body position can be varied, make adjustments so that the center of the axis of the cam is directly aligned with the center of the joint that is being exercised.
- Do not twist or move your body during the exercise.
- Maintain a loose, comfortable grip with your hands.
- Begin with a weight that can be handled comfortably for 8 repetitions.
- For cardiorespiratory conditioning, move quickly from one machine to the next.
- Compound and double machines are designed to use a single joint exercise to pre-exhaust a muscle and then a multiple joint exercise to cause a further state of exhaustion on the same muscle. Example: On the compound leg machine, perform the leg extension to the point of momentary failure, then immediately perform the leg press.

The major exercises which can be performed on Nautilus machines include:

1. Hip Extension
2. Leg Extension
3. Leg Press
4. Leg Curl
5. Heel Raise
6. Ab-Ad Exercise
7. Foot Flexion
8. Arm Cross
9. Decline Press
10. Parallel Dip
11. Chin Up
12. Pullover
13. Behind Neck Pulldown
14. Side Lateral Raise
15. Overhead Press
16. Shoulder Shrug
17. Two Arm Curl
18. Tricep Extension
19. Abdominal Curl

DUO/POLY HIP AND BACK MACHINE
HIP EXTENSION

Major Muscles Involved: Gluteus maximus, spinal erectors

Description of Exercise:

- Lie on your back with your legs over the roller pads.
- Align your hip joints with the center of the rotation cams.
- Fasten the seat belt snugly around your waist and grasp the handles lightly.
- Extend both your legs at same time and push back with your hands.
- Hold one leg in a fully-extended position and allow your other leg to bend up and back as far as possible.
- Extend your bent leg downward until it is even with the extended leg.
- Arch your lower back and force both legs downward.
- Pause, repeat the same action with your other leg.

Important Points:

- When your legs are fully extended in a contracted position, keep your knees both straight and together and point your toes downward.
- When one leg is bending backward in the negative movement, do not allow your extended leg to raise upward.

Hip and back: starting position

Hip and back: pause position

COMPOUND LEG MACHINE
LEG EXTENSION

Major Muscles Involved: Quadriceps

Description of Exercise:
- In a seated position, place both of your feet behind the roller pads with the back of your knees against the front of the seat.
- Adjust the seat back so that it touches your lower back.
- Keep your head and shoulders against the seat back throughout the exercise.
- Raise your feet until both legs are straight.
- Pause, recover to the starting position and repeat.

Leg extension: pause position

Leg extension: starting position

COMPOUND LEG MACHINE
LEG PRESS

Major Muscles Involved: Gluteus maximus, quadriceps

Description of Exercise:
- Flip down the foot pads.
- Place your feet on the pads with your toes turned slightly inward.
- Push both of your legs outward until your knees are almost straight.
- Pause with your knees slightly bent, slowly recover to the starting position and repeat.

Important Points:
- Move immediately from the leg extension to the leg press.
- Relax your hands, neck, and face muscles during the exercise.

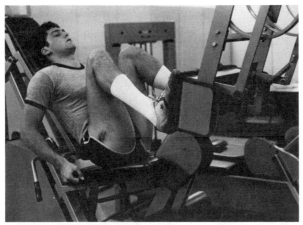

Leg press: starting position

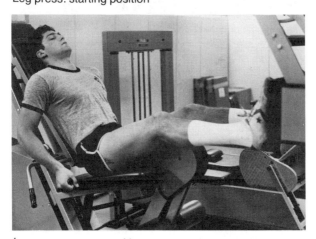

Leg press: pause position

LEG CURL MACHINE
LEG CURL

Major Muscles Involved: Hamstrings

Description of Exercise:
- Lie face down on the machine.
- Place the back of your ankles under the roller pads with your kneecaps just off the end of the bench.
- Grip the handles loosely.
- Curl your legs upward and attempt to touch your buttocks with the roller pads.
- Pause, slowly recover to the starting position.

Important Points:
- Your feet should be flexed with your toes pointing towards your knees throughout the exercise.
- Allow your hips to rise off of the bench when nearing full contraction.

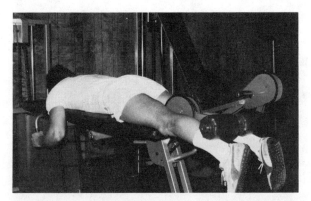

Leg curl: starting position

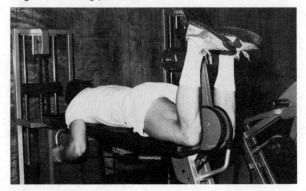

Leg curl: pause position

MULTI-EXERCISE MACHINE
HEEL RAISE

Major Muscles Involved: Calves

Description of Exercise:
- Adjust the belt comfortably around your hips.
- Place the balls of your feet on the first step with your hands on the top step and your back parallel to the floor.
- Keep your knees locked throughout the exercise.
- Raise your heels as high as possible.
- Pause, slowly recover to the starting position and repeat.

Important Points:
- Do not lean forward.
- Attempt to flex your toes upward at the bottom of the movement to allow for a maximum stretch.

Heel raise: starting position   Heel raise: pause position

 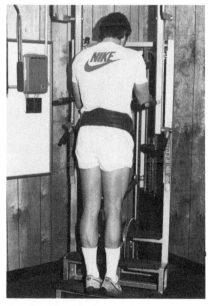

HIP ABDUCTION/ADDUCTION MACHINE
HIP ABDUCTION

Major Muscles Involved: Gluteus medius

Description of Exercise:

- Adjust the lever on the right side of the machine until both movement arms are together.
- Move the thigh pads to the outer position.
- Sit in the machine and place your knees and ankles on the movement arms. Your outer thighs and knees should be firmly against the resistance pads.
- Spread your knees and thighs to the widest possible position and pause.
- Return slowly to the starting position and repeat.

Important Point:

- Keep your head and shoulders relaxed against the back seat throughout the exercise.

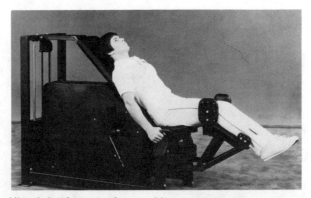

Hip abduction: starting position

Hip abduction: pause position

HIP ABDUCTION/ADDUCTION MACHINE
HIP ADDUCTION

Major Muscles Involved: Adductor magnus

Description of Exercise:

- Adjust the level on the right side of the machine until the movement arms are as wide as comfortably possible.
- Move the thigh pads to the inside position.
- Sit in the machine and place your knees and ankles on the movement arms. Your inner thighs and knees should be firmly against the resistance pads.
- Press your knees and thighs smoothly together and pause.
- Return slowly to the starting position and repeat.

Important Point:

- Keep your head and shoulders relaxed against the seat back throughout the exercise.

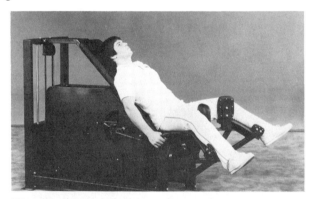

Hip adduction: starting position

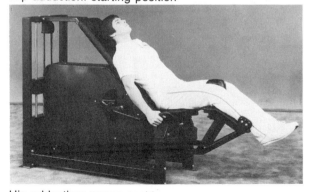

Hip adduction: pause position

LEG CURL MACHINE
FOOT FLEXION

Major Muscles Involved: Tibialis anterior

Description of Exercise:

- In a seated position, place throo cushions under your calves and place your toes under the roller pads.
- Keep your torso in a vertical position and grip the sides of the bench loosely.
- Curl your toes up towards your knees as far as possible.
- Pause, slowly recover to the starting position and repeat.

Important Points:

- Allow your feet to extend completely on the negative part of the movement.
- As an exercise which exercises the antagonist muscle group of the calves, the foot flexion should always be performed when the heel raise is performed.

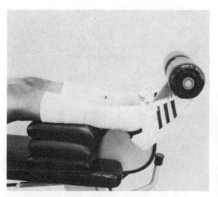

Foot flexion: starting position

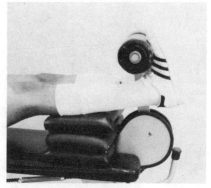

Foot flexion: pause position

DOUBLE CHEST MACHINE
ARM CROSS

Major Muscles Involved: Pectoralis major, deltoids

Description of Exercise:

- Adjust the seat until the center of your shoulders is directly beneath the center of the overhead cams.
- Fasten the seat belt.
- Place your forearms behind the movement arm pads.
- Grip the handles loosely (use whichever handle will place your elbow at a 90° angle).
- Keep your head and shoulders back and push your elbows together until the movement arms touch.
- Pause, slowly recover to the starting position and repeat.

Arm cross: starting position   Arm cross: pause position

DOUBLE CHEST MACHINE
DECLINE PRESS

Major Muscles Involved: Pectorals, deltoids, triceps

Description of Exercise:
- Use the foot pad to bring the handles forward.
- Grip the handles with an overhand grip and remove your feet from the pad.
- Push the handles forward until your arms are extended.
- Pause with your elbows slightly bent, slowly recover to the starting position and repeat.

Important Points:
- Perform the decline press immediately after completing the arm cross.
- Keep your head and shoulders against the seat back throughout both movements.

 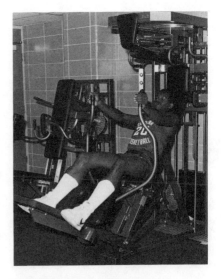

Decline press: starting position   Decline press: pause position

MULTI/EXERCISE MACHINE
PARALLEL DIP

Major Muscles Involved: Pectorals, deltoid, triceps

Description of Exercise:

- Adjust the carriage high enough so that your knees will not hit the steps during the exercise.
- Climb the steps and suspend your weight with your elbows locked and your knees bent.
- Slowly lower your body until your elbows are less than a 90° angle.
- Recover to the starting position by extending your arms until your elbows are straight.
- Pause, repeat.

Parallel Dip: starting position

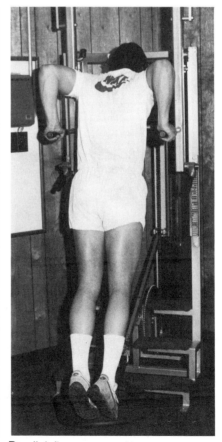

Parallel dip: pause position

MULTI/EXERCISE MACHINE
CHIN-UP

Major Muscles Involved: Latissimus dorsi, biceps

Description of Exercise:
- Place the crossbar in a forward position and adjust the carriage to a point where your chin is just over the bar when you are standing on the top step.
- Grasp the crossbar with an underhand grip and suspend your weight with your arms straight and your knees bent.
- Pull your body upward until your chin is over the bar.
- Pause, slowly recover to the starting position and repeat.

Important Points:
- Negative-only repetitions of chin-ups (and dips) can be performed with or without the use of the belt.
- When performing negative-only repetitions, begin in the starting position, slowly lower your body, taking approximately four seconds, then climb the steps and repeat.

Chin-up: starting position

Chin-up: pause position

SUPER PULLOVER MACHINE
PULLOVER

Major Muscles Involved: Latissimus dorsi

Description of Exercise:
- Adjust the seat so that the center of your shoulder joints are aligned with the center of the cams.
- Fasten the seat belt tightly.
- Depress the foot pedals to move the elbow pads forward.
- Place the back of your elbows on the pads.
- Your hands should be open and leaning against the groove in the curved portion of the bar.
- Remove your feet from the foot pedals and allow your elbows to move back slowly to a stretched starting position.
- Rotate your elbows forward and downward until the crossbar touches your hips.
- Pause, slowly recover to the starting position and repeat.

Important Points:
- Keep your head and shoulders against the seatback throughout the exercise.
- Keep your hands open and relaxed throughout the exercise.
- Allow your elbows to stretch back as far as possible at the completion of each repetition.

Pullover: starting position   Pullover: pause position

TORSO ARM MACHINE
BEHIND NECK PULLDOWN

Major Muscles Involved: Latissimus dorsi, biceps

Description of Exercise:
- Adjust the seat low enough so that your arms are fully extended when resistance is felt.
- Fasten the seat belt tightly.
- Lean forward and grasp the handles with your palms facing inward.
- Pull back and downward until the base of your neck is touched.
- Pause, slowly recover to the starting position and repeat.

Important Points:
- Be sure that your arms are fully extended when the negative movement is completed.
- Lean forward throughout the exercise.

Behind neck pulldown: starting position   Behind neck pulldown: pause position

DOUBLE SHOULDER MACHINE
SIDE LATERAL RAISE

Major Muscles Involved: Deltoids

Description of Exercise:

- Adjust the seat so that the center of your shoulder joints is aligned with the center of cams.
- Fasten the seat belt.
- Place the back of your wrists on the pads and grip the handles loosely.
- Raise your elbows until your arms are parallel with the floor.
- Pause, slowly recover to the starting position and repeat.

Side lateral raise: starting position   Side lateral raise: pause position

DOUBLE SHOULDER MACHINE
OVERHEAD PRESS

Major Muscles Involved: Deltoids, triceps

Description of Exercise:
- Grasp the handles behind your shoulders.
- Straighten your arms overhead.
- Pause, slowly recover to the starting position and repeat.

Important Points:
- Perform the overhead press immediately after the side lateral raise.
- Keep your legs over the end of seat.
- Do not arch your back.

Overhead press: starting position   Overhead press: pause position

NECK AND SHOULDER MACHINE
SHOULDER SHRUG

Major Muscles Involved: Trapezius

Description of Exercise:

- Take a seated position and place your forearms between the pads.
- Keep your palms open and facing upward.
- Straighten your back so that the weight stack is lifted. If you cannot lift the weight stack in this position, place one or more cushions on the seat.
- Raise your shoulders as high as possible.
- Pause, slowly recover to the starting position and repeat.

Important Points:

- Do not lean back or use your legs during the exercise.
- Do not straighten your arms.
- If available, watch yourself in a mirror while performing this exercise in order to ensure that you are doing the exercise correctly.
- Relax your facial muscles while performing the exercise.

 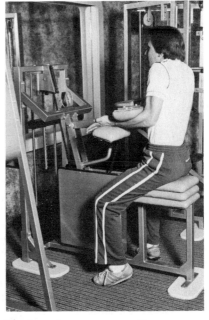

Shoulder shrug: starting position   Shoulder shrug: pause position

MULTI CURL MACHINE
TWO ARM CURL

Major Muscles Involved: Biceps

Description of Exercise:

- Assume a seated position, and place your elbows on a pad aligned with the center of the cams.
- Curl both of your arms until your wrists are just in front of your neck.
- Pause, slowly recover to the starting position and repeat.

Two arm curl: starting position

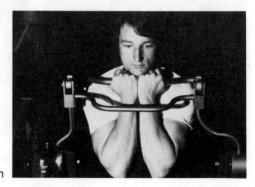

Two arm curl: pause position

MULTI CURL MACHINE
TRICEP EXTENSION

Major Muscles Involved: Triceps

Description of Exercise:
- Assume a seated position and place your elbows on a pad aligned with the center of the cams.
- Extend both of your arms until your elbows are straight.
- Pause, slowly recover to the starting position.

Important Points:
- Keep your back and head in a vertical position.
- Insure that your arms reach are held momentarily in a fully extended position while in the pause (mid-range) position.
- This exercise can also be performed by alternating one arm at a time.

Tricep extension: starting position   Tricep extension: pause position

ABDOMINAL CURL

Major Muscles Involved: Rectus abdominis

Description of Exercise:

- Adjust the seat so that the lower part of your sternum is even with the lower edge of the top pad.
- Place your ankles behind the roller pads.
- Spread your legs and sit erect.
- Grasp the handles and keep your elbows high.
- Your head and shoulders should remain against the pad.
- Shorten the distance between your rib cage and your navel by contracting your abdominals.
- Pause in the contracted position, return to the starting position and repeat.

Important Point:

- Don't pull with your arms or lift up with your legs.

Adbominal curl: starting position

Abdominal curl: pause position

7
STRETCHING

Flexibility was defined in Chapter 3 as the functional capacity of a skeletal joint to move through a normal range of motion. The degree of flexibility of specific joints is effected by the connective tissue surrounding that joint. This includes ligaments (attach bones together), tendons (attach muscle to bone), and muscle (causes movement of the joint). Ligaments are slightly extensible but do not have a great deal of elasticity. Since muscle tissue on the other hand has a degree of elasticity, "stretching" muscle tissue permits more efficient joint movement. Elasticity refers to the amount of movement (stretch) the tissue can incur when force is applied and then returned injury-free to its resting length. Extensibility is the amount the tissue can stretch without resulting in damage. For muscle tissue this amount is approximately 50%.

An organized stretching program should always be supervised by the coaching staff in order to ensure that it is done properly. Every practice session and pre-game warm-up should begin with at least 5-10 minutes of stretching. Such a session not only helps to develop and sustain an athlete's level of flexibility, but also enables the athlete to warm-up sufficiently before engaging in the intensive efforts typically part of each practice. In order to maintain flexibility, flexibility exercises should be included in the year-around conditioning program. It is extremely important that the stretching program be well organized since any time wasted on the court can always be better spent on more productive endeavors.

In order to achieve maximal results, an athlete should adhere to the following principles when performing flexibility exercises:

- Perform each movement in a slow, deliberate manner. Any bouncing or jerking may lead to injury.
- Perform every exercise properly. Performing the exercise incorrectly only compromises the results.
- Start with a slow easy stretch and continue the stretch to the point of a slightly painful, burning sensation, hold in that position, then recover.
- Repeat the same exercise attempting to stretch a little further.
- Begin each stretching session with a light jog to increase the circulation of the blood to the muscles.
- Perform each exercise 6-8 times.

All stretching exercises should be performed slowly, without bouncing or jerking.

FLEXIBILITY EXERCISES

BEND AND REACH

Area Stretched: Lower back, Hamstrings

Description of Exercise:
- Stand with legs straight and feet shoulder width apart.
- Torso vertical with hands on hips.
- Slowly bend forward at the waist and reach for the ground behind the feet.
- Hold for 8 counts, recover to starting position and repeat.

Important Points:
- Bend slowly and **do not bounce**.
- Attempt to touch ground behind feet.
- Attempt to stretch further on second repetition.
- Do not allow knees to bend.

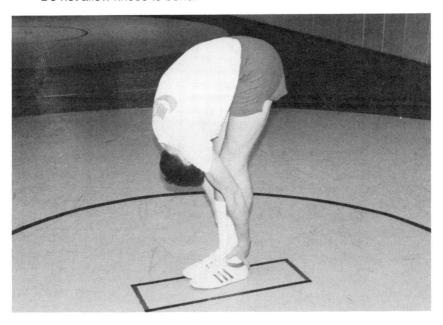

Bend and reach

TOE TOUCH

Area Stretched: Lower back, hamstrings, calves

Description of Exercise:
- Stand with legs straight and feet together.
- Torso vertical with hands on hips.
- Slowly bend forward at the waist and touch hands to the ground.
- Hold for 8 counts, recover to starting position and repeat.

Important Points:
- Bend slowly.
- Keep legs straight.
- Do not bounce.

Toe touch

LATERAL HIP AND GROIN STRETCH

Area Stretched: Hips, hamstrings

Description of Exercise:

- Stand with left leg extended to left side, toe pointing forward and inside of foot touching ground.
- Right foot pointing to right, right knee bent and right hand on right thigh.
- Torso vertical.
- Bend right knee with torso upright until maximum stretch occurs on left hip.
- Hold for 8 counts, recover to starting position and repeat.
- After the stretch is completed on one leg do the same exercise with opposite leg.

Important Points:

- Keep extended leg straight.
- Extend leg far enough to the side to allow maximum stretch.
- Do not bounce.
- Keep torso vertical.

Lateral hip and groin stretch

ACHILLES AND CALVE STRETCH

Area Stretched: Calves and achilles tendon

Description of Exercise:
- Bend right knee and extend left leg as far back as possible with ball of foot on ground.
- Keeping left leg straight slowly lower left heel down towards ground.
- Hold for 8 counts, recover to starting position and repeat.
- When completed do same exercise with opposite leg.

Important Points:
- Keep left leg straight.
- If heel touches ground extend leg further back.
- Lower slowly as the achilles tendon can be easily injured with a jerky motion.

Achilles and calve stretch

HURDLERS HAMSTRING STRETCH

Area Stretched: Hamstrings

Description of Exercise:

- Assume seated hurdlers position with left leg extended, right knee bent, right toes pointed straight back and torso vertical.
- Slowly bend forward at waist.
- Touch nose to knee while reaching with both hands for heel of extended foot.
- Hold for 8 counts, recover to starting position and repeat.
- When exercise is completed perform same exercise with opposite leg.

Important Points:

- Keep extended leg straight.
- Bend forward slowly and recover fully between repetitions.

Hurdlers hamstring stretch

WALL STRETCH FOR CALVES

Area Stretched: Calves, achilles tendon

Description of Exercise:

- Place palms on wall and lean against wall at at least a 45° angle.
- Extend both legs as far back as possible keeping balls of feet on ground.
- Slowly lower heels down towards ground.
- Hold for 8 counts, recover to starting position and repeat.

Important Points:

- Keep both legs straight.
- If heels touch ground extend legs further back.
- Lower heels slowly.

Wall stretch for calves

HURDLERS QUAD STRETCH

Area Stretched: Quadriceps, hips

Description of Exercise:
- Assume seated hurdlers position with left leg extended, right knee bent, right toes pointed straight back and torso vertical.
- Slowly twist torso sideways as far as possible .
- Hold for 8 counts, recover to starting position and repeat.
- When exercise is completed perform same exercise with opposite leg.

Important Points:
- Keep bent knee in contact with ground.
- Use hands for support when leaning backwards and recovering to starting position.

HIP ROTATOR STRETCH

Area Stretched: Lower back, buttocks, hips

Description of Exercise:

- Lay on back with arms extended to sides at shoulder level.
- Extend both legs.
- Bend left knee and rotate across right side of body.
- Grasp left knee with right hand and pull knee downward and up toward right shoulder until maximum stretch is felt.
- Hold for 8 counts, recover to starting position and repeat.
- When exercise is completed perform same exercise with opposite leg.

Important Points:

- Keep left shoulder flat on ground throughout exercise.
- Keep right leg extended.

Hip rotator stretch

SEATED HAMSTRING STRETCH

Area Stretched: Lower back, hamstrings

Description of Exercise:
- Sit with both legs extended slightly wider than shoulder width apart.
- Bend forward at waist attempting to touch nose to ground and at same time reach both hands to feet.
- Hold for 8 counts, recover to starting position and repeat.

Important Points:
- Avoid, fast, bouncing movement.
- Keep legs straight.

Seated hamstring stretch

SEATED HAMSTRING AND CALVE STRETCH

Area Stretched: Lower back, hamstrings, calves

Description of Exercise:
- Sit with both legs extended and heels together.
- Bend forward at waist attempting to touch nose to ground and at same time reach both hands to feet.
- Hold for 8 counts, recover to starting position and repeat.

Important Points:
- Avoid fast, bouncing movement.
- Keep legs straight.
- Keep feet flexed for greater calve stretch.

Seated hamstring and calve stretch

PARTNER GROIN STRETCH

Area Stretched: Groin

Description of Exercise:

- Sit with knees bent, soles of feet touching each other, and heels pulled in toward groin.
- Partner kneels in front with hands on inside of partner's knees.
- Partner slowly pushes knees down until maximum stretch is experienced.
- Hold for 8 counts, recover to starting position and repeat.

Important Points:

- Partner should apply slow, steady pressure.
- Partners must communicate so that proper amounts of pressure is applied.

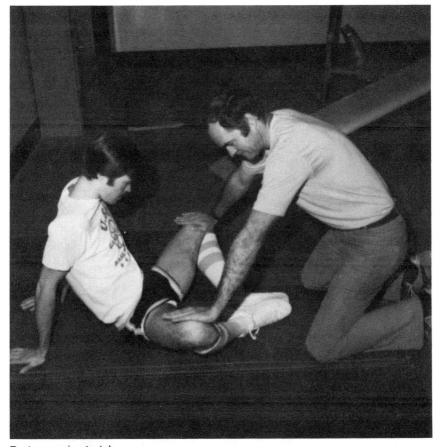

Partner groin stretch

PARTNER CHEST STRETCH

Area Stretched: Shoulders, pectorals

Description of Exercise:

- Sit on ground with legs extended, hands interlaced behind head and elbows back.
- Partner stands behind with side of one leg supporting partner's back and hands on inside of partner's elbows.
- Partner stretches elbows back to point of maximum stretch with a slow deliberate movement.
- Hold for 8 counts, recover to starting position and repeat.

Important Points:

- Partners must communicate so that the correct point of tension is reached.
- Bring elbows completely forward between repetitions.

Partner chest stretch

PARTNER SHOULDER STRETCH

Area Stretched: Shoulders, pectorals

Description of Exercise:

- Sit on ground with legs extended, hands interlaced behind head and elbows back.
- Partner stands behind with side of one leg supporting partner's back and hands on inside of partner's elbows.
- Partner stretches elbows back and then upward to point of maximum stretch with a slow deliberate movement.
- Hold for 8 counts, recover to starting position and repeat.

Important Points:

- Partners must communicate so that the correct point of tension is reached.
- Bring elbows completely forward between repetitions.

Partner shoulder stretch

STANDING-PARTNER HAMSTRING STRETCH

Area Stretched: Hamstrings

Description of Exercise:

- Standing on right leg, raise left leg forward to waist level, toes pointing upward and heel resting in partner's hands.
- Bend forward at waist and attempt to touch nose to knee.
- Hold for 8 counts, recover to starting position and repeat.
- When exercise is completed perform same exercise with opposite leg.

Important Points:

- Keep both legs straight throughout entire exercise.
- Extended leg should be held at waist level or higher.

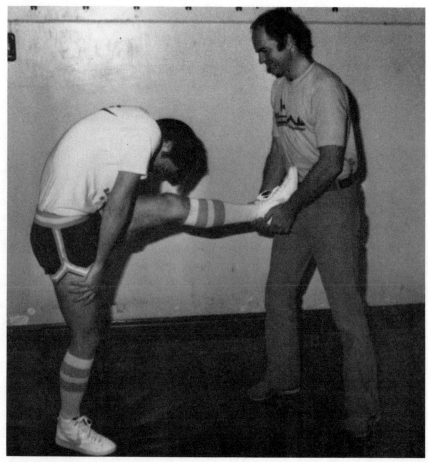

Standing partner hamstring stretch

STANDING-PARTNER GROIN STRETCH

Area Stretched: Hamstrings, groin

Description of Exercise:

- Standing on right leg, raise left leg forward to waist level, toes pointing to the right and foot resting in partner's hands.
- Bend slowly over right side and attempt to touch palms to ground in front of right foot.
- Hold for 8 counts, recover to starting position and repeat.
- When exercise is completed perform same exercise with opposite leg.

Important Points:

- Keep both legs straight throughout entire exercise.
- Extended leg should be held at waist level.

Standing-partner groin stretch

8
DEVELOPING
AEROBIC FITNESS

A erobic fitness is a "must for any conditioning program designed to help improve performance on the court. As mentioned earlier in Chapter 3, the cardio-respiratory system of an athlete's body (heart, lungs, and circulation network) is the vehicle which transports oxygen to his muscles and at the same time carries the byproducts of energy production (carbon dioxide, etc.) to the lungs for expulsion from his body. Basically, the efficiency with which this system transports these gases determines his "wind" or stamina on the court. If an athlete "runs out of gas" on the court, it's probably because his transport system has simply not been conditioned properly. This system, much like an individual's skeletal muscles, responds to stress by getting stronger or more efficient. Therefore, when an athlete runs and stresses his cardio-respiratory system, it responds by becoming more efficient. As a result, an athlete would have more "stamina" to meet the rigorous demands of playing basketball.

Just as an athlete's routine for developing muscular fitness is sport specific, his running program should be sport specific. That is to say, it should be made up of prolonged submaximal effort-running (aerobic) as well as short maximal effort-sprinting (anaerobic). His muscular system can be very highly developed but, without a very efficient transport system to get oxygen to the muscles, his performance cannot be sustained at a sufficiently high level throughout an entire game. I recommend to our athletes that they run with court performance in mind—almost every day—during the pre- and off-seasons.

We use a variety of methods to develop aerobic fitness. Each athlete is encouraged to run several miles on his own, as many mornings a week as possible. Weather permitting, running hills is another aerobic exercise performed by our athletes. In addition, we suggest that our athletes play 2 full court basketball games at least three times per week during the pre-season. During the five weeks immediately preceding the mid-October start of organized practices, we require our athletes to run a minimum of five days per week. Each succeeding week, we ask them to run for a longer minimum period of time during each run (Table 8-1).

1st week — 24 minutes

2nd week — 28 minutes

3rd week — 32 minutes

4th week — 36 minutes

5th week — 40 minutes

Table 8-1. Minimum amount of time required per run

STRESS

Running is stressful. The underlying principle of all conditioning efforts is adapting to stress. Adaptation refers to the fact that the body increases its resistance to stress through previous exposure to stress. Developed by Hans Selye and articulated into what is called a "general adaptation syndrome," this concept as applied to running means that an individual should run followed by a suitable recovery period for the adaptation to that stress to occur, followed by another stress and recovery, etc., gradually increasing the stress as the body's adaptation increases. If an athlete goes beyond his capacity to adapt, his body will incur some form of break-down such as severe exhaustion. One of the primary elements of any effective conditioning program is to determine proper doses of stress and recognize the symptoms of over- and under-stressing.

PRINCIPLES OF AEROBIC IMPROVEMENT

In order to develop his level of aerobic fitness in the most effective and efficient manner possible, an athlete should closely adhere to the following five principles:

- Substantial **demand** must be placed on the cardiovascular system. In general, a heart rate of 140-160 beats per minute for 12-15 minutes should be achieved 4 to 5 times per week.

The underlying principle of all conditioning efforts is adapting to stress.

- As much of the body's **total musculature** as possible should be involved in the activity.
- The activity must be at a level of **intensity** which will produce an appropriate demand on the cardiovascular system. Intense, but not too intense. A heart rate of 140-160 beats per minute will suffice. A general guideline is that the running should be stressful but not so demanding that an athlete couldn't carry on a conversation while running.
- The activity should be engaged in for a period of **duration** long enough to generate improvement. At least 12-15 minutes per run is required.
- The activity should be **regular**. Four to five times a week is a guideline for developing a conditioning base. Once an adequate level of cardiovascular fitness is achieved, it may be maintained with slightly fewer weekly workouts.

In order for aerobic improvement to occur, an appropriate demand must be placed on the athlete's cardiovascular system.

An aerobic program should involve aerobic activities lasting at least 12-15 minutes consecutively.

1. Marathon
   - Long, relatively slow running at 60-80% of max.
   - 95%aerobic, 5% anaerobic
   - Quantity, not quality
   - Can be viewed as a series of intervals with no recovery period
2. Fartlek
   - Swedish word for speed play.
   - Unstructured workout
   - Long run with changes of pace; everything from sprinting to jogging.
   - 80% aerobic, 20% anaerobic
3. Interval
   - Fastest conditioner over a short period
   - Can do more work with less fatigue because of rest period.
   - Increase stroke volume many times during a workout; i.e., after each bout.
   - Do not allow full recovery.
   - 55% aerobic, 45% anaerobic
   - Overload principle
   - Specificity of training
4. Repetition
   - Run closer to all out each repetition.
   - Allow near full recovery; bout #1 does not affect bout #
   - 75% anaerobic, 25% aerobic
   - Distance may be longer than in interval training.
5. Spring
   - All out exercises bouts of short duration.
   - Allow full recovery between bouts.
   - 95% anaerobic, 5% aerobic
   - High speed, high resistance

Table 8-2. Five Basic Types of Running Programs

ANAEROBIC FITNESS

A comprehensively planned "running" program should focus not only on the development of aerobic fitness (wind, stamina, etc.) but also the development anaerobic fitness (the ability to more forcefully for short periods without oxygen). In a sport such as basketball where there is constant sprinting up and down the court, often for extended periods of time, anaerobic fitness is particularly important.

Anaerobic power for a basketball player is developed through two methods: (1) increasing the level of muscular fitness of the muscles involved in the various basketball skills; and (2) engaging in activities which involve anaerobic fitness, for example interval training.

TYPES OF RUNNING PROGRAMS

Table 8-2 lists the five most traditional types of running programs. As can be seen, there is no program which involves strictly aerobic fitness or strictly anaerobic fitness. Each of the five classifications of programs approaches the five training variables (speed of runs; distance run; number of runs per training session; the amount of recovery between the runs; and the type of recovery between the runs) somewhat differently. Depending upon how a coach wants to mix the five variables will influence what running program he uses. At one time or another, either in practice or as part of the general conditioning regimen, we involve our athletes in all five types of programs.

TESTING AND EVALUATION

To motivate our athletes and to aid in evaluating the level of progress from their conditioning efforts, we test our athletes once a week during the preseason on both the mile run and the quarter mile run. The mile run involves aerobic fitness almost exclusively, while the 440 emphasizes anaerobic fitness to a greater degree than aerobic fitness. Both tests are conducted on the running track by our senior manager. As much as possible, testing conditions are standardized from week to week. Results are posted on the team bulletin board—this is an excellent motivational aid.

9
DEVELOPING
AGILITY

There are a number of basic motor skills which play an important role in determining how successful an athlete will be at his sport. Each sport requires different levels of compentencies at these basic motor skills. For basketball, two of the most important of these motor abilities are agility and response time. This chapter discusses how to develop agility, while Chapter 10 examines response time.

Agility is the ability of an individual to change directions rapidly and effectively while moving at a high rate of speed. In a fast moving sport, such as basketball, a high level of agility can frequently make the difference for an athlete between being a champion or an also ran. Many of the factors influencing an individual's level of agility are beyond the influence of the athlete himself (genetics, etc.). Two steps, however, can be taken to develop an athlete's level of agility to its fullest potential: (1) by conditioning (developing the systems of the body involved in the movement) and (2) by practicing the skill (developing the neuromuscular efficiency involved in the movement).

The list of agility drills is almost endless. Coaches and athletes can use their imagination to develop their own. At the University of South Carolina, we structure our agility program to emphasize an athlete's ability to "touch and go." "Touch and go" refers to the ability of an athlete to immediately take off after making momentary contact with the floor. This ability requires a supple and fluent movement on the part of the athlete—a capability obviously beneficial to basketball players.

PRINCIPLES OF IMPROVEMENT

If the athlete wants to maximize his level of agility, he should closely adhere to the following principles:

- Practice activities involving agility.
- Place a demand upon the systems of the body involved.
- Accuracy and speed should be combined in equal amounts.
- Distributed (versus massed) practice provides the optimum level of improvement (this means that it is better to practice 3 times a day for 10 minutes each time than one time for 30 minutes).
- Repetition is essential.
- Don't push past the point of fatigue.

AGILITY DRILLS*

The Single Circle Drill:

- **Purpose:** To develop the two foot takeoff with restricted base and the ability to change posture in air: balance during flight.
- **How to do:** One foot in and one out of the circle (Note: The circle may be a tire, plastic hula hoop, etc.); jump up into tuck position; switch feet on landing. Touch and go. Repeat for 30 seconds.

| Jump | Back Straight | Touch & Go | Toes Pointed |
| | | | Repeat Sequence |

The single circle drill.

*Developed with the assistance of Dr. Rudy Mueller, East Stroudsburg State College (Pa.)

Bench Drill (Top of Swedish Box or similar object):

- **Purpose:** To develop one leg takeoff and change flight posture.
- **How to do:** One foot on bench and one on floor. Push off top leg and switch leg positions to opposite side of box. Touch and go. Repeat for 30 seconds.

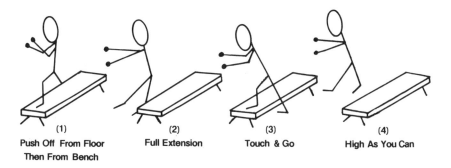

(1)	(2)	(3)	(4)
Push Off From Floor Then From Bench	Full Extension	Touch & Go	High As You Can

Bench drill.

Defensive Triangle Drill:

- **Purpose:** To develop defensive slides with changes of direction, approach and retreat.
- **How to do:** Starting at top tire, use diagonal retreat slides (lead foot really pronounced out in front) to tire; pivot on lead foot and defensive horizontal slide (as if playing the dribbler) to tire and then use "approach" step up to starting tire—then repeat, going to either side. Stay down low on defense—use of hands.

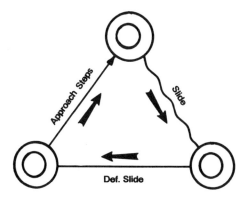

Defensive triangle drill.

180° Double Circle Drill (Circles tied together next to each other):

- **Purpose:** To develop twisting, posture in air.
- **How to do:** One foot in each circle, jump, turn 180° and land with one foot in each circle. Repeat for 30 seconds. Jump-turn 180° touch and go—turn again.

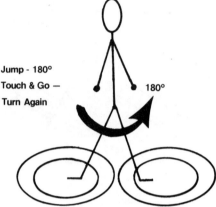

180° double circle drill.

Diagonal Rope Drill (Two or more 15-20 foot ropes tied 4 feet at highest and slanting to floor where it is weighted down with 25 lb. weight):

- **Purpose:** To develop two foot take off over various heights of rope.
- **How to do:** Standing with side to rope and starting at low end, jump sidewards. Continue to progress up the ropes higher and higher until you decide it's as high as you can go. Jump backwards down the rope. Touch and go. Repeat for 30 seconds.

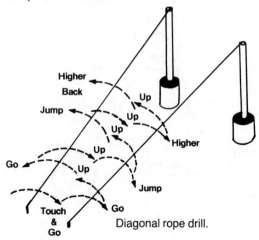

Diagonal rope drill.

Four Circle Drill:

- **Purpose:** To develop change of direction upon landing and immediate take-off.
- **How to do:** Start with two feet inside rear circle—jump forward into circle—jump sideward into circle—jump backward into circle—and jump sideward into original circle. Touch and go. Repeat for 30 seconds.

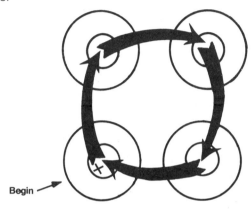

Four circle drill.

Crazy Leg Drill (Two circles tied together next to each other)

- **Purpose:** To develop the control of body momentum when take-off and landing are on one leg—crossing midline.
- **How to do:** Start by putting right leg in left circle, bring left leg in front of you and put in circle—continue this action, using touch and go. Repeat for 30 seconds.

Crazy leg drill.

Straddle Jump Drill:

- **Purpose:** To develop two foot take-off with extended base.
- **How to do:** Legs either side of tire; jump up into air and touch toes. Return to straddle position. Touch and go. Repeat for 30 seconds.

Straddle jump drill.

10
DEVELOPING QUICKNESS (RESPONSE TIME)

Response time is the required time for an individual to **initiate a response** to a specific stimulus and to move part of his body from one point to another. Coaches frequently refer to this motor skill as "quickness." Obviously, this is a highly valuable trait for basketball players. Similar to agility, the only productive methods for improving an athlete's level of response time are conditioning and specificity training.

PRINCIPLES OF IMPROVEMENT

In order to maximize his level of response time, an athlete should closely adhere to the following principles:

- Place a demand on systems involved.
- Regular practice is required.
- To a certain extent, the development of "quickness" is substantially inhibited by specific genetic limitations.
- Develop the involved musculature (weight training).

RESPONSE TIME DRILLS

- **Two Ball Wall Drill** — stand 5 feet or less away from wall, take two balls and bounce one at a time against the wall. The pass and catch is always with two hands (2 hand chest pass).
- **Back to Wall** — stand 5 feet or less from wall with your back to the wall. Throw the ball directly over your head and shoulders, jump, turn, and catch the ball in front you. At the moment of catching the ball, you should be completely facing the wall.

Quickness can only be developed in individuals to a limited degree. To a large measure, either an athlete is born with quickness or he doesn't possess this vital motor skill. Quickness drills can help, however, refine the skill.

- **Partner Wall Throw** — standing 5 feet or less from wall and facing it. Your partner will throw the ball from behind you off the wall. You should catch it as it rebounds and before it hits the ground. Immediately upon catching ball, flip it over shoulder to thrower and get ready.
- **Call Ball** — stand with back to the passer. Passer passes ball with varying heights and speeds and at some point he calls name of receiver who turns around, locates ball, and catches it. Balls of all sizes and weights.
- **Listen for Bounce** — stand with back to the passer—passer bounces ball, receiver turns to catch ball when he hears the bounce. Receiver should turn in proper direction—vary speed, distance and flight. Ball must be able to bounce.
- **Back to Back** — two athletes stand back to back in defensive stance, one individual flips, drops, or rolls ball toward front of the other who, upon hearing or seeing it, moves to get it at the nearest spot. Caution: Don't let the ball bounce up high before getting it, must go down with hand to get it.
- **Circle Rotation** — circle of 6 players about 20 feet in diameter with one player in the circle. Each player on outside of circle has a ball, the man in the center slowly circles on a spot with hands at his sides. Players in the outer circle pass ball to center man as he faces them, but at their own discretion. Center man must return ball and keep turning or reverse the turn.

THE AUTHOR

A sportswriter once described University of South Carolina head basketball coach Bill Foster as "the All-American Coach." Foster's record over 22 years certainly bears out that classification.

Foster has won more than 350 games while establishing a reputation as a rebuilder of collegiate basketball programs. He served stints as head coach at Bloomsburg State, Rutgers, Utah and Duke before coming to South Carolina in March 1980.

Foster's teams have played in the National Invitation Tournament three times and the NCAA championship tournament three times, his Duke team in 1978 advancing to the national championship game. That showing earned him National Co-Coach of the Year honors from the National Association of Basketball Coaches as well as Coach of the Year honors from *The Sporting News* and *Playboy* magazine. He was also Atlantic Coast Conference Coach of the Year.

Foster is listed in *Who's Who in America*; served as president of the National Association of Basketball Coaches, 1975-76; was elected to the National Basketball Hall of Fame's Board of Trustees in 1978; is a charter member of the Elizabethtown College Sports Hall of Fame; and was inducted into the Pennsylvania Sports Hall of Fame in 1979.

A native of Norwood, Pa., he is a 1954 graduate of Elizabethtown College with a 1957 Master's degree from Temple University. While a student at Elizabethtown College, Foster earned four letters in basketball and three in soccer. He is married to the former Shirley Junkin of New Cumberland, Pa., and they have four daughters.